T0068100

# My Journey down the Reincarnation Highway

# My Journey down the Reincarnation Highway

*The True Story of a Man Who*
*Found Nine of His Past Lives*

FRANK MARES

iUniverse, Inc.
Bloomington

My Journey down the Reincarnation Highway
The True Story of a Man Who Found Nine of His Past Lives

Copyright © 2012 by Frank Mares

All rights reserved. No part of this book may be used or reproduced by any means, graphic, electronic, or mechanical, including photocopying, recording, taping or by any information storage retrieval system without the written permission of the publisher except in the case of brief quotations embodied in critical articles and reviews.

iUniverse books may be ordered through booksellers or by contacting:

iUniverse
1663 Liberty Drive
Bloomington, IN 47403
www.iuniverse.com
1-800-Authors (1-800-288-4677)

Because of the dynamic nature of the Internet, any web addresses or links contained in this book may have changed since publication and may no longer be valid. The views expressed in this work are solely those of the author and do not necessarily reflect the views of the publisher, and the publisher hereby disclaims any responsibility for them.

Any people depicted in stock imagery provided by Thinkstock are models, and such images are being used for illustrative purposes only.

Certain stock imagery © Thinkstock.

ISBN: 978-1-4759-5924-6 (sc)
ISBN: 978-1-4759-5925-3 (hc)
ISBN: 978-1-4759-5926-0 (e)

Library of Congress Control Number: 2012920562

Printed in the United States of America

iUniverse rev. date: 11/13/2012

# Contents

# Introduction

*Not only is the universe stranger than we imagine, it is stranger than we can imagine.*

— J. B. S. Haldane

I know that you are not reading this book because it's a best seller. And unless you are a relative or someone else who knows me, you probably came across this book because you were led to it by coincidence or some strange circumstance. Strange coincidences are more normal than you might believe. Coincidence is actually a force in the universe that guides us. Since you are here, I ascertain that someone important wants you to read this book because it's going to help you in some way. I myself was guided by coincidence to a book that started all of my supernatural adventures, and these adventures in turn led me to discover reincarnation and the spirit world.

If you knew my soul's background, you would undoubtedly agree that I should be one of the last people in the world to share this story. I used to be an atheist in this life, and in a few of my past lives, I was a villainous criminal. For example, in my life as Nicholas, I was once considered the most dangerous man in Europe, but surprisingly, history remembers me instead as the "thief." I stole so many wagons full of booty that I bought a castle with my ill-gained fortune. Besides stealing, I also took several innocent lives with my sword and pistol during that wild time. Luckily for me, I was not punished back then for my heinous crimes because I was a highly connected nobleman. My social rank was so high that I eventually rose to the highest levels of the imperial court in my older years. Punishment for my sins was to be delivered only after I died—350 years ago.

The life of Nicholas was not the only one in which I was a nobleman who lived sinfully. I was once an extremely powerful man with a renowned reputation for treachery in the 1200s. Through my underhanded actions, other powerful, rich people found themselves locked in my dungeon begging for mercy. I was known as Konrad then, whom history records as being both extremely aggressive and angry. A modern interpretation of those traits would be that I had medieval anger management problems. In boring contrast today, I am a fifty-five-year-old man living in the Columbus, Ohio, area. I have a family and own two businesses that provide me with a very nice living. However, in this life, I am no longer famous, angry, powerful, or dangerous. I no longer have these traits, because they do not fit into my current life's grand plan.

How is it possible that I could have been these three different men? How did I even come to know these unbelievable things? The answers to these questions are found within these pages. That is, I found out that reincarnation is reality not just for me but for everyone. This information came to me during a spiritual journey that I started in 2009. It started out innocently enough—its original goal was to find out if there really was something beyond death other than eternal, unconscious darkness. Going into the journey, I had no expectations, and I certainly did not believe in reincarnation. I never expected to enter the "Twilight Zone," but I did. What launched my journey into the realm of the supernatural was that I started to meditate twice a day. Through meditation I developed a minor psychic ability that allowed me to access information that is not available to most mortals.

As time went on, I kept the existence of my Twilight Zone world secret, telling only my wife, Karol, what was happening. She was horrified that people might look at us differently if I broadly shared my discoveries and stories. Later, I shared my psychic stories outside of my marriage for the very first time with my brother-in-law, Jeff, at a restaurant bar. Despite my secrecy, stories leaked out to Karol's family, and Jeff was curious about what I was doing. He is a traditional Catholic, and I thought he would change the subject after he heard a few snippets of my experiences. (Most people with deeply held beliefs do not want to hear about nonorthodox things.) Instead, I was surprised to find him deeply engaged in my stories, and he kept egging me on to tell him more. To my amazement, he was fascinated rather than dismissive. As I had been living these experiences on a day-to-day basis and had not been looking at them as an outsider would, I came to the realization that there actually was an interesting, coherent story in what I was experiencing. It was at that point that I started to record my experiences for a possible book, long before this journey actually ended.

In this book, you will go right along with me as we jointly uncover the mysteries of the spirit world and reincarnation. I want to assure you that everything in this book is true and was experienced by me. The only thing that is not accurate is my last name, although my real first name is Frank. Karol was insistent that our names be changed to protect our privacy and business reputations.

Before we start this journey, you need to understand that the purpose of this book is to tell you how I found reincarnation, what I actually did in my prior lives, and more important, *why* I lived these particular lives. We will spend a lot of time communicating with spirits because, in these conversations, many little factoids and confirmations of the reincarnation process are revealed in an offhand manner. This is not a textbook, so I am not going to go into any deep explanations about the mechanics of reincarnation. If you want that information, I provide a list of reference books that you can study. I do promise you that you will learn many surprising things by reading these chapters. In the end, you might not believe me. If you don't, that's okay; I am not on a mission to covert anybody to a new belief system. However, if you do not believe me now, you will believe me after your current body closes its eyes for the last time.

# Chapter 1: Frank, the Atheist

*Fervid atheism is usually a screen for repressed religion.*
—Wilhelm Stekel

## Reincarnation highway mile marker: USA, 1976

I could start this story at the same point that I did when I told it to my brother-in-law, which was the time that I started to meditate. But, instead, I will use the late spring of 1976 to begin. It's the perfect place to start because it really shows where my level of spirituality was for most of my life, a measurement that would read a big fat zero on the religious scale.

Let me set the scene. I was a twenty-year-old college student sitting with my girlfriend, Michele, in a priest's office. Michele was a slender, pretty, eighteen-year-old blonde who was a devout Catholic—so devout that she went to a weekly church youth group meeting every week besides going to Mass. We had met at the grocery store where we both worked part time and had been dating steadily for five months. Her parents absolutely did not like me—no, make that they could not stand my presence. I tried to get along. I schmoozed her mother like crazy, but my charms were not moving her. It's not that I was not a nice guy with prospects, but the issue was that I was not Catholic. I was not even a Christian. I had no religion, as I had a live-and-let-live attitude. I believed that religion was everyone's personal choice, and I respected other people's beliefs. However, my attitude about respecting other people's beliefs was not shared by all people, especially Michele's parents. Regardless, she was my first love, and I was really into this girl. So if she wanted us to meet with a priest, I would go along like a good little boy. Why did she want us to meet the priest? It seems that I threw her into a minor spiritual crisis when I told her about the logical paradoxes of Christianity. It wasn't my fault; she challenged my lack of beliefs one night and asked me to explain them. Two years previous, when I was a high school senior, I had read a book called *The Case against God*. It presented a devastating string of logic that just shot holes through Christianity like a machine gun. Since she had challenged my lack of belief in a mocking manner, I shared some of this counterlogic with her. The experience rocked her; she just could not resolve the paradoxes that the book posed. This was the first time in her life that she had ever heard a different viewpoint. In response, she went to her priest and asked the same questions that I had presented her with. When she did, I am sure that alarm bells started ringing down the halls of St. Anthony's parish. Hence, the priest asked for a meeting with the both of us to straighten out the situation. He cautioned me during the meeting that when I had these types of questions, I should ask someone who is trained to answer them. Well, even though I was young and stupid, I knew that my relationship with Michele was moving from thin ice to slushy water. She was emotionally connected to me, but her parents would use any excuse to get rid of me. I planned to be perfectly good during the meeting and was not going to be combative. I just wanted to get through this crisis with a minimum of damage. Nevertheless, the priest couldn't do any better than Michele had in addressing the questions, and he eventually retreated behind the "all will be revealed after you leave this life and that is why you need faith" routine. I thought, *What a copout. You can't even defend your own beliefs logically.* Needless to say, my romantic relationship with Michele ended not long after this meeting, when her parents forbade me from entering their house. Unfortunately, the pain of our breakup would linger as I would continue to work with her at the store. Eventually, Michele married and moved out of state.

So how did I become an atheist in the first place? Blame it on my parents. They were not religious, and my mother, who was raised a Catholic girl, just could not buy its dogma. She left the religion quickly after she left her childhood home. Growing up in my parents' household, I never had the religious training (or brainwashing, some would say) that other kids received, much to the horror of my beloved Italian Catholic grandmother, Naomi. She who would cringe when my parents would call out, "Don't let the bed bugs bite" rather than recite the Lord's Prayer before bed. To rectify the situation, she would occasionally sneak me into mass when I was little. To her disappointment, these occasional church visits never resulted in the religious seed sprouting within me. Looking back, I believe that my lack of religious indoctrination allowed me to examine things objectively. I could study history and science, compare them to religious beliefs, and see the obvious discrepancies. This ability to be objective reinforced my lack of belief, which I learned over time to keep "below the radar" so I wouldn't be a social outcast. However, having reached the dating age, my heresies were starting to be exposed.

What were the barriers that kept me from being a Christian or otherwise religious as an adult? Let's keep it simple. Solve these two paradoxes, and I will believe in God.

1. *If God is truly loving and perfect, why is there evil in this world and why do the innocent suffer?* This is probably the most commonly discussed dilemma of them all. Why would the horror of the Holocaust ever be allowed to happen? Why is there so much suffering and unhappiness in life? Why is life so difficult? If we have only one shot at life, shouldn't it be idyllic and happy? I really do not believe that most people have a happy life. You have your ups and downs, but it seems that there are more downs. Who do you know of that has a perfect life? If you can think of a specific person, you may consider that he or she may have a better life than you, but is that life without pain? I am willing to bet that that is not the case.

2. *Why can't I directly see or experience God or the supernatural?* If God is the creator of the universe and the driving force that keeps it going, why can't we see even a glimmer of the supernatural at work? Or why doesn't God or his angels communicate with us directly?

My hard-core lack of belief in a higher power and the spiritual world is "square one" of my story. Philosophers have been grappling with these two tough issues for thousands of years without any measurable success. You have to admit that I have created a very high standard that must be met before I could ever believe that God exists. Barriers can be overcome, and you will come to see how the spirit world reintroduced itself to my soul despite the overwhelming obstacles I had set up. This reunion had to happen because spirituality is the whole foundation of reincarnation.

# Chapter 2: The Homing Beacon

*Being obsessional does not necessarily mean sexual obsession, not even obsession for this or for that in particular; to be obsessional means to find oneself caught in a mechanism, in a trap increasingly demanding and endless.*

—Jacques Lacan

## Reincarnation highway mile marker: USA, 1960s

I went through my boyhood in the 1960s. What is relevant about that period is that, despite being remembered as the hippie age of Aquarius, it was also the decade that the American men who fought in World War II reached their midforties. These men were in their prime earning years, and the TV networks created shows in hopes that they would attract their attention, such as *The Gallant Men*, *Combat*, and the comedy *Hogan's Heroes*. You can still see these shows on the retro sixties cable channels. If you watch them, you will notice that they all featured brave American soldiers who fought the Germans in World War II. These black-and-white wartime dramas were usually set in France, and the lack of color on the TV screen made the German soldiers look especially ominous as their uniforms were dark gray. Dark colors always signified the bad guys. Looking back on it now with older eyes, the shows were really not that good. But as a ten-year-old, I thought they were great and watched them every week. Even though the Germans were the bad guys, I always admired them. The American soldiers, in contrast to the Germans, seemed to be dressed slovenly and always needed a shave. The Germans had cool-looking uniforms with high collars and black, polished boots. They were always disciplined and looked sharp, and their weapons were fearsome with their nasty black submachine guns and their fast-firing big machine guns. The German officers were always tough and professional, and their subordinates would immediately jump into action at their orders. As a boy, I frequently wondered why these German troops lost every week when they looked so much better and seemed tougher than the Americans. When my friends in the neighborhood would play army with toy guns, I never minded playing the German side. I just wished I could have a plastic gray German helmet so that I could play the part better.

One strange thing was my youthful reaction to the show *Hogan's Heroes*, which was based on the outlandish plot that Allied prisoners in a German World War II prison camp had a secret underground complex beneath their prisoner barracks. From this complex, they would conduct sabotage and spy operations, causing mayhem deep within Germany. The German officers in the show were presented as complete buffoons and were easily manipulated by their prisoners. Even at the young age of ten, I thought this show was insulting to the Germans as it made them out to be complete morons. For some reason, I almost felt personally insulted. Another thing I noticed specifically about *Hogan's Heroes* was that the German officers were always threatening their subordinates with assignment to the Russian front. Conversely, being sent to the American front was never mentioned as a punishment. By implication, that Russian front must have been a real bad place.

In junior high and high school, I took German for my language class. Our school system back then offered only Spanish, French, and German language courses, no Chinese or Japanese like today. A strange fact is that although I took German for only three years, I can still speak some of it thirty-seven years later. My grammar is horrific, but if I traveled to Germany, I know that I could get around okay. How did I keep my fluency? Wherever I took a job in my college and banking days, there was always a middle-aged German lady working in the same department as I worked. Even when I started my own business, I still managed to have a German-speaking woman on my staff. I had an impulse to speak German, and I would talk to those ladies in their native language to indulge my compulsion. They often mistakenly assumed that I had come from a German family; but my family's background was Italian and Czechoslovakian. The only German blood in my ancestral line comes from one great-grandmother, whom I have never met.

Another unusual thing I remember was my desire to wear coats modeled after the World War II German military tunic, the kind that had four pleated pockets on the front. My mom custom made a winter coat in that style for me when I was eighteen, but that particular style was never fashionable where I was. When I was twenty, I marched around in a German brown-shirt tunic outfit at a college Halloween party.

From the age of ten on, my typical reading has been World War II history; I never stopped studying the subject. I had consumed hundreds of World War II books by the time I reached my forties. One of my more interesting memories is from a novel that told the story of what some Japanese civilians experienced during the atomic bomb attack on Hiroshima. In particular, I remember the story of a young Japanese woman who was out in the open when the atomic explosion occurred. She was not close enough to be killed immediately, but she was badly burned. After the attack, she walked, dazed, with a large group of survivors in a burning part of the city. The flames drove the survivors to a river and to a bridge that crossed it. The bridge formed a bottleneck, and the press of people caused her to fall off the bridge and into the water. Unfortunately for this character, she could not swim, and she sank below the surface and drowned. Her religion was Buddhism, a common religion in Japan, where reincarnation is accepted and believed. Her last thought as she was losing consciousness was, *I hope my next life is better.* That line really struck me. Having grown up in Western society, I had never given any thought to what reincarnation would really mean. This dying woman was not panicking that her only life was ending, but rather she was hopeful that when (not if) she came back, she would be in a happier life. I considered her dying hope a very comforting thought, although I had never actually believed that reincarnation could possibly be real. To me, it was just a nice, dramatic touch in the book.

By the time I reached my late forties, my reading interests had shifted specifically to the German-Russian front in World War II. Most people do not realize that most of the big WWII battles occurred in Russia. That was where the real action was. Germany had 80 percent of its men allocated to the Russian front and used the remaining 20 percent to fight the Americans and British. I would read many, many firsthand accounts of the German military survivors of these battles. The stories of loss, suffering, and hardship were amazing as far as what these men endured. I thought there was no way that I, personally, could survive long in those conditions. Thank God, I never had to go through that hell.

With all of my readings about and fascination with World War II, the ironic thing was that I, a man in his midforties, had never shot a firearm—BB and paintball guns, yes, but real guns, no. I guess I had never had the opportunity as my dad did not own a gun and we did not live in the country. But I always dreamed of shooting the German submachine gun, the MP-40. Until I was forty-four, I had only seen this gun in movies or pictures in books. I finally saw and actually touched one when I was serving on a grand jury in Cleveland, Ohio. One day, the lawyers took the jury on a tour of the police crime lab. In one room of the lab, technicians tested the identifying characteristics of bullets from individual guns. On the wall of the lab, all by itself, hung a German MP-40 submachine gun! Obviously, it must have been confiscated from someone who had brought it back from the war. It was a big thrill to see one up close and touch it.

I finally lost my gun virginity in a big way. A year after the birth of my twins, my in-laws were kind enough to watch the babies while my wife and I took a four-day trip to Las Vegas to recover from the first year of twin infancy. While I was in our hotel room, I noticed a flyer advertising a nearby gun range that offered an opportunity to shoot a variety of submachine guns—one of which was an actual German MP-40! I excitedly told my wife that I had to go there. She was extremely apprehensive, thinking that I would shoot myself or that there would be an accident. I assured her that I would not do it unless it was safe. The next morning, while she slept in, I took a cab to the gun range. I walked into the place and saw an amazing arsenal of guns hanging on the wall behind the counter. I asked how the process worked and was told that a gun range employee would assist me in the indoor range and watch over me. That sounded safe enough for me! I bought three clips of ammo and was outfitted with safety glasses and ear protection. Then, I followed the employee into the indoor gun range in the next room.

The shooting range had a dark, claustrophobic basement feeling. A series of separated stalls were set up for people to shoot from, aiming at paper targets. Before entering the range, the attendant cautioned me to shoot slowly and to not let the gun shoot on full automatic, explaining that the gun was getting old and had a tendency to jam. He carried the MP-40 to an open stall. I was disappointed that their rules allowed only the gun-range attendant to insert the ammo clip and cock the gun. After he had done those, he handed the black and dangerous-looking gun over to me and stepped back out of the shooting stall. With great delight, I examined the weapon, looking over every detail. I then shouldered it and let loose a rapid single-shot barrage of nine-millimeter lead at the paper target about twenty feet away. I was immediately comfortable with this gun; it felt like I had been shooting it for years. (Ho-boy, if I had only known the real story about this at the time!) It was easy, and I was pretty good, right on target. I quickly went through two clips of ammo (sixty rounds), and when the attendant loaded my last clip—I couldn't help it—I let loose on full automatic. When shooting on automatic, the barrel tends to rise with each shot because of the rapid recoil of the gun. The stream of bullets rose, and I sawed off the clip that was holding the target to the wire down range. The attendant was pissed, but oh, well. That was too much fun. After I was done, I gave the gun back and took a cab back to my hotel. There, I excitedly told Karol about my experience. She didn't understand why it was a big deal, but she was happy for me.

*The MP-40 submachine gun.*

Fast forward to the age of fifty—the business that I had established with Karol really started to take off to the point that I had money to buy "toys" or start a collection. I don't know why or how it started, but I received a monthly mail catalog called *The Sportsman's Guide* that offered good deals on sunglasses, clothes, and shoes. Every quarter, the company would also send a military-surplus edition, offering, among other things, old European military paraphernalia and occasionally old submachine gun parts to be reassembled into display pieces. They would not sell all of the parts needed to make the guns fully functional, just enough to create a nonfunctional display piece. I ordered an Italian submachine gun, which I then assembled into a display piece. As my attention was turning to actual guns instead of books, I stumbled across websites that sold German Mauser rifles from the war.

The Mauser 98-K rifle was the standard rifle of the German soldier in WWII. For some reason, I had to have a Mauser rifle that came from the Russian front. (Don't ask me why; shooting or possessing guns was never one of my desires.) I ordered an eastern-front Mauser from a special website and hung it on my wall in the basement. It was to be the first piece of what would become a large collection of German guns used on the eastern front.

*The Mauser 98-K, Otto's and Frank's first rifle*

I then discovered the eBay of the gun world—www.gunbroker. com. You can find almost any gun being sold on the used market on that site. And lo and behold, the site was selling German MP-40 parts kits. I could finally have my own MP-40! I bought my first one for a price that my wife would kill me over, but I finally had my own. Next, I bumbled across the opportunity to buy my first assault rifle, the German MP-44. Then I was able to procure another MP-40 at an auction and two Russian PPSh-41 submachine guns. Why would I have Russian submachine guns in my collection? German soldiers captured thousands of these particular guns and used them for themselves. Some German WWII newsreels include glimpses of German soldiers holding the PPSh-41. I then expanded my collection further when I noticed that GunBroker.com also auctioned WWII memorabilia. For some reason,

I had always wanted a German Iron Cross, so I bought one, as well as a German wound badge and a German medal that was given to the survivors of the first winter in Russia, which the Germans jokingly called the frozen meat medal. Finally, having just read the story of a German soldier who was trapped with his army on the Kurland (also Courland) Peninsula, hundreds of miles behind the Russian front, I bought the last decoration awarded by the German army in 1945, the Kurland arm cuff band. I displayed the medals and the arm band on the wall in my downstairs "man cave," a wall that had become quite full. My family christened the collection area the "gun room," and I had a light installed in the ceiling to highlight the collection. Then I stepped back and asked myself, *What the heck am I doing? I am a patriotic American. If I'm going to collect guns, why haven't I collected American guns? Why would I collect guns at all? I was not a soldier!* I was stunned with the sudden realization that I had just created a shrine to German soldiers on the eastern front, and I had no idea why I had done it. Little did I know then that the specific placement of the guns and medals on the wall symbolically told an actual story from World War II. This shrine also had another purpose; it was to function as a "homing beacon" so that I could find my way back to my past.

*Frank's strange shrine to the German soldiers of the eastern front*

# Chapter 3: Searching for Immortality

*When a friend dies, it's something of you who dies.*

—Gustave Flaubert

*Surely God would not have created such a being as man, with an ability to grasp the infinite, to exist only for a day! No, no, man was made for immortality.*

—Abraham Lincoln

## Reincarnation highway mile marker: USA, 2005

During my atheist years, I really hated going to funerals. I hated everything about them. For example, I always cringed at the silly comments people would make about how good the deceased looked in his casket. *Really?* I would think. *He really looks like a hideous wooden doll.* I was also frequently at a loss as to what to say to the widow. She had to have heard the word *sorry* about a thousand times that day, and I never believed that my saying the thousand and first *sorry* would help her at all. In most eulogies, someone would make the declaration that the deceased was watching this service by looking down upon us from heaven. That sounded good, but I knew better—*The deceased is really in that big box over there, and he no longer has the ability to look at or pay attention to anything.*

Since I hated going to funerals in general, imagine my feelings about going to the funeral of a loved relative. It's the one experience that I absolutely dreaded and feared. Unfortunately, saying a permanent good-bye to a loved one cannot be avoided if you live long enough. My first close loss was at the age of seventeen. My eighteen-year-old cousin Ted had died when his Army barrack balcony collapsed in a freak accident. He had a military funeral, and it was beyond unsettling to me as this was the closest Death had ever come to me at that point in my life. Death then made a habit of saying hello to me at least once every decade after Ted's death. Each new decade would bring me the loss of someone who was very close to me. Loss number two was the death of my Italian grandfather, Frank, to cancer when I was twenty-two. I had always loved him deeply. I admired my immigrant grandfather for his accomplishments and was profoundly grateful for his kindness to me. He was a big part of my childhood, and his loss was very difficult to endure. Then, I was in my midthirties when my Italian grandmother, Naomi, also died of cancer. She had been my emotional mother in this life, and we were extremely close. She had wanted so much to see and be with my children, but she saw that it was not to be as she neared death long before they were born. The best she could do was to make a colorful needlepoint unicorn on a child's pillowcase so that some part of her would be with my kids. Currently, that pillowcase has a revered place on my daughter Jani's bed.

The last and most painful loss was my father when I was forty-eight. My dad and I had always been close. People just loved him; he was one of those special leaders that people have the privilege to encounter in life. The following illustrative story sums up how people felt about him.

At the end of my dad's sales career, one-third of the Yellow Pages salesmen in Ohio reported to him through a number of sales managers. Most of his subordinate sales managers had been brought up from the sales ranks and then developed and mentored by my father. He retired in 1990 and died in 2005, but I happened to encounter one of his subordinates in 2011 in a checkout line at a local store. I noticed the man because he was wearing a Yellow Pages promotional jacket, a jacket that I had not seen for years. I just had to ask him if he knew my dad. When he found out whom I was, tears actually came to his eyes when he recounted how he had first heard of my father's death six years before. These sentiments about my father were common. People liked him and wanted to be around him. I felt the same way; I liked being around him because he was always fun and was a great practical joker.

He always encouraged me, and he was always there to help me through life's rough spots.

My dad loved to pilot airplanes; that was always a big part of his life. He owned a number of small airplanes from his twenties on and actually retired to the famous Spruce Creek community in Florida, where everyone lived directly on the grounds of a private airport. At his house in that community, he parked his favorite airplane, a Beechcraft Bonanza, in his aircraft hangar behind his house. That was his heaven on earth.

Dad had absolutely no medical issues until he was diagnosed with pancreatic cancer at the age of sixty-six. I knew then that most people die quickly after this diagnosis, often within six months. I was absolutely devastated when he told me the news in person at my house in Ohio. In the weeks after he announced his illness, I could see that he was following a path to a quick end. He was in a lot of pain, and he was weak. Fortunately, Karol's massage therapist, Kathy, told her of an herbal remedy called essiac tea that was popular in Canada, saying that it had saved her mother from colon cancer after her doctors had given up on her. After researching essiac, Karol convinced my dad to try it. It was a good thing that he drank the tea because it seemed to work. Although he complained about the taste and the grittiness of it, he absolutely skated through his chemotherapy and radiation treatments. His doctors were amazed that he had so few side effects from the cancer treatments. Best of all, his pain was almost completely eliminated, and he resumed a normal life. The only change was that he wasn't allowed to fly his airplane alone anymore, but he got around that prohibition by making sure that one of his friends was in the front seat with him. His doctors were amazed by the lifestyle that he was able to maintain.

However, about two years after his diagnosis, his health started to decline again. He put the word out to the three of us kids that it was time to come to Florida to say good-bye. I was stunned; I couldn't believe that he could be in such a bad state. After all, I had been golfing with him only six months before. *He must have stopped taking his essiac,* I assumed.

After getting this news, Karol and I made arrangements to take our family to his home in Daytona. The morning after I arrived, I went alone to see him at the hospital. I had not seen him for six months, and I was shocked at his appearance. He had that gaunt, cancer-patient look that my grandfather had had just before he died. He did not have the strength to get out of bed. I knew deep down that it was the end, but I wasn't ready to accept it. We spent most the day together, saying good-bye. For two guys who were not known for crying, we sure did cry a lot. During our conversations, he told me that he did not want to go, that he wanted to know how things would turn out in the future. I did not know what to say to that; all I could say to him was that he had lived a good life and that he should be thankful for all that it gave him. I left in the late afternoon promising to bring my family to visit him the next day.

The next day was a Sunday, and I took Karol and the kids to the hospital. Jani, my daughter, looks very similar to my sister, Chris, and when four-year-old Jani walked into Dad's hospital room wearing a pretty white hat, he broke into sobs. Because of his illness and the distance he lived from us, my dad had never really had a chance to develop a relationship with my kids. It appeared that he was developing an attachment to Jani at this late stage, and I was sad it was happening too late. At the end of our visit, we all kissed him good-bye, Jani being the last one to do so. We promised to be back the next day, and my mom stayed with Dad at the hospital that night. However, he died that night.

My family returned to Florida six weeks later to attend a large memorial service held for my father in a big hangar at Spruce Creek. Hundreds of people were there. A special part of the service was a flyby of an acrobatic airplane team performing the missing man formation. Another pilot was flying my father's Bonanza in the formation, and as part the maneuver, he pulled up and away from the formation and to the west, where the sun sets. As my father's plane headed west, I said, "Good-bye, Dad," out loud. We then returned to Columbus, sad.

There is nothing like the death of a parent to force one to look into death's deep, dark abyss. One of the disadvantages of being an atheist is that you have no hope when you contemplate the subject of death. For us, once your eyes close for the final time, that's it—game over. Nothing is left but a dreamless sleep that you do not experience or remember and that you do not wake from. When you are young, the best way to deal with that kind of reality is to go into denial and not face it. Well, denial was no longer an option for me. It was my time to start to reconcile with my mortality.

As some consolation for our loss, my wife and I would comment about how our son Brian was a clone of my father—same skull shape, same facial features, same hair, same personality. Brian has tremendous drive to get what he wants, just like my dad. He also has to be constantly occupied or else he gets bored, just like my dad. Brian was just four years old when my dad died, so he had no real time to spend with him to pick up his mannerisms. After his death, we noticed that Brian started to re-create my dad's quirky mannerisms. For example, he would whistle (badly), just like my dad had when he walked down the hall. When my dad would sit, he would sometimes cross his legs like a woman would, and Brian started to do the same thing when sitting in a chair or his car seat. When my dad would nap, he would curl up on the couch with his hands tucked together, prayer-like, between his knees, and Brian started to do the same thing. One day, Brian turned to his sister Jani and said out of the blue, "You can't do that because you're a girl!" This was the same line that my dad would use when he wanted to rile a woman. Brian had not learned the phrase from me; I work in an all-female company and would be killed if I ever breathed such a thing. As time went on, Brian's sudden adoption of my dad's mannerisms after his death was starting to become slightly unnerving rather than consoling.

I didn't know—maybe I was starting to think too much of Brian's uncanny similarities to my father. But then a very strange event happened about three months after Dad's death. I was carrying Brian out to the van to take him to day care. I sat him down in his car seat and started to buckle him up. I just happened to be looking at his face as I was adjusting his straps. Just then, my dad's face appeared, transposed over Brian's face! The image of my dad's face was silver in color and had a blank look. It appeared for just half a second, but it was there, and then it just disappeared. I startled when I saw that vision and lurched backward. *What the hell was that?* I thought. *Was that real, or am I imagining things?* I went back inside and told Karol what I had seen. "Wow, that's weird," she said. This incident would lodge in her memory because she was able to recall it later. I eventually filed away that experience as the first hallucination in my life and continued to wrestle with questions about mortality.

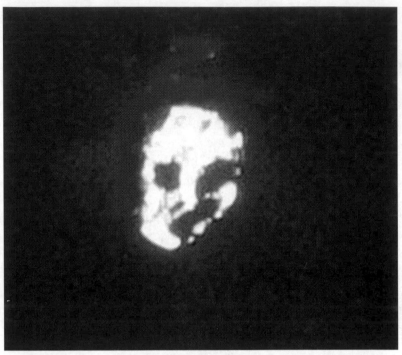

*This picture was captured during a ghost hunt by my friend Judy. My dad's face during his garage appearance looked very similar to this but was much more detailed. Photography by Judy Bodenhamer.*

The more I thought about mortality, the more I believed that my dad's, or anybody's, death did not make logical sense. Why would people go through a difficult life in which they start from nothing, learn everything through painful mistakes, and then have their hard-won lessons just flushed away at the end? It would be just a huge waste of time and effort if nothing was saved from a lifetime of experience. In nature, nothing is wasted; everything is recycled. So why would experience and knowledge be wastefully destroyed? It seemed to me that this destruction would be a violation of the natural order, and this idea was making me realize that maybe my current belief system was missing something. Just as I had rejected Christianity because it was not logical, it occurred to me that the idea that death was strictly the end could also be illogical. But no other explanation that I knew of made sense either. I resolved to try to find an answer to this paradox.

I had to delay my pursuit of this answer for four years, however, because Karol and I were involved in a lawsuit against the State of

Ohio to try to save our special medical billing business. This battle took every bit of our mental and emotional energy. This story alone would be material for another book, but I will skip the details here. It was a grueling and stressful four years, but we prevailed and our business was saved. Once our life got back to normal, I had the luxury of turning my attention back to the issue of mortality. But where would I start?

I started first by studying the subject of human consciousness. I chose this starting point because consciousness is what you appear to lose when you die. Does consciousness really die with you, or does it go somewhere? But first of all, what is consciousness?

Go to a mirror and look at yourself. You see your image with your eyes. Your eyes function like cameras, projecting your image onto an internal screen inside your head. But who inside your head is looking at that internal screen and recognizing that that image is you? The answer is that it is your consciousness. If a dog looked into the same mirror, he would just see another dog. He does not recognize himself, but you do. Being able to recognize yourself in a mirror is evidence of what is called being self-aware. Humans, apes, elephants, and whales are self-aware; all other earth animals are not. What happens to your self-aware consciousness when you die? Atheists say it expires with your death. Christians say that it goes either to heaven or hell depending on how good you were, and Buddhists and Hindus say that your consciousness is recycled into a new body. It was at this point that I realized that consciousness is the soul that Christians talk about. It was embarrassing that it had taken me so long to make this connection.

Some people think that your consciousness is not a soul or a spiritual entity. Some of these people theorize that you could have immortality if you stuffed all of your memories into a hard drive and then lived on inside a computer. Let's say I could transfer everything in my mind to a computer hard drive. The idea, then, would be that I would start seeing the world through a camera attached to the computer. But how would I transfer my consciousness to the computer? At what point would my conscience leave my body and then exist in the computer? How would anyone do this? The theorists don't address these questions. I think the answer is that you cannot transfer your consciousness to a machine because your consciousness is not made up of just your memories and thinking ability. It has to be much more than that, but what I did I really know? So, to find that answer, I actually ordered a college course on CD-ROM that had twelve lectures on the concept of consciousness. The course was taught by a college philosophy professor, and I was fascinated to learn about all the different viewpoints about consciousness. However, by the end of the course, I had concluded that there were no definitive answers as to how a person's consciousness comes into existence, how it works, or where it goes after death. It's amazing that something that humans live with every moment of their waking lives is taken absolutely for granted and yet cannot be definitively explained. At the conclusion of the course, I realized that the main question that must be answered is, what happens to your consciousness after you die? At that point in my life, I was finally open to any logical idea that could answer that question.

When you are open to things, things seem come to you. One of the great things about the Internet is that you have all kinds of information at your fingertips. Through some online browsing, I learned about the work of Dr. Ian Stevenson, who documented a great number of case studies in which children around the ages of three and four actually remembered dying suddenly in a previous life. Their memories included details about who they were, what they did for work, who their families were, and where they lived. Dr. Stevenson believed that his research proved that these memories were actually real and not fantasies. However, Dr. Stevenson's case studies have been disputed by other scholars, and whether these memories are real, I certainly don't know. However, I then found a story that was widely reported in the news media in 2004 and that supported Dr. Stevenson's work.

The story concerned a little boy in Louisiana named Jimmy who recalled prior life memories of being a World War II American fighter pilot. From the age of two, Jimmy had an obsession with airplanes although his parents were not pilots or associated with airplanes in any way. When young Jimmy would play with his toy airplanes, he would seemingly display expert knowledge about them that was far beyond what a four-year-old would know. For example, he would be able to tell the difference between bombs and drop fuel tanks or that Corsair fighter planes had a tendency to get flat tires when landing on aircraft carriers. After a while, Jimmy experienced many nightmares that he described as "airplane crash on fire, little man can't get out." When his parents asked him what had happened to his airplane, he said that it had crashed and caught fire and that the Japanese had shot his plane. Flipping through a book, the two-year-old pointed at a picture of Iwo Jima in the Pacific and said that was where his plane had been shot down.

To help Jimmy with his nightmares, his parents took him to a counselor who had Jimmy share his memories with her. He was able to recall the name of an aircraft carrier called *Natoma Bay* and the name of a pilot he claimed to have flown with, a Jack Larson. Jimmy also said that his plane had sustained a direct hit on the engine. Strangely, Jimmy had also begun signing his crayon drawings "James 3." With this information, Jimmy's dad did extensive research. Much to their surprise, his parents found that there really was a small American aircraft carrier named the *Natoma Bay* and that one of the pilots who flew off of that carrier was named Jack Larson. Jimmy's dad talked to a few pilots who had served on the *Natoma Bay* and learned that the only pilot from the squadron who had been killed at Iwo Jima was named James M. Huston Jr. Ralph Clarbour, a rear gunner on a bomber that flew off the Natoma Bay, says his plane was right next to one flown by James M. Huston Jr. during a raid near Iwo Jima on March 3, 1945. Mr. Clarbour said he saw Huston's plane struck by anti-aircraft fire. "I would say he was hit head on, right in the middle of the engine," he said. James M. Huston Jr. was shot down while on his 50th mission, his last before he was due to go home. His father describes his reaction to this information as, "Holy mackerel! You could have poured my brains out of my ears. I just couldn't believe it!"

Jimmy's parents, Bruce and Andrea Leininger, wrote a book about this experience called *Soul Survivor: The Reincarnation of a World War II Fighter Pilot*. As I had absolutely no explanation for consciousness, I reasoned that these reincarnation stories could be just as viable as any other explanation. And as an atheist, I could be justified in considering reincarnation as real based upon the laws of physics. The logic goes like this: There is an empirical law of physics called the law of conservation of energy. It states that the total amount of energy in an isolated system remains constant over time (is said to be *conserved* over time). *A consequence of this physics law is that energy can be neither created nor destroyed.* Many consider consciousness to be a high form of energy. No one has proven this to be true yet, but if it is, then consciousness could not be destroyed by death. This, then, may explain why consciousness, in the example of little Jimmy from Louisiana, could jump from the dead pilot to Jimmy. Holding onto this bit of logic, I was open to more information about reincarnation. Once again, coincidence led me further down this road.

Because I love books and bargains, I occasionally go to bookstores to browse the discount section. A few days after reading about young Jimmy, the reincarnated WWII pilot, I went to a Borders bookstore to look around. Prominently on display next to the discount area was the book *Life after Death: The Burden of Proof* by Deepak Chopra. Well, that title certainly caught my eye! I picked up the book and read the back cover, where I saw the question, "What happens to the spirit after the body dies?" It then continued, "Deepak Chopra draws on cutting-edge scientific discoveries and the great wisdom traditions to provide a map of the afterlife." *This is just what the doctor ordered!* I thought. I quickly bought the book and drove home to read it. I found it interesting; it was a mixture of Hindu mythology told in the style of childhood stories, recounted by Chopra. The mythological stories were combined with modern scientific theories that supported the idea of immortal consciousness and reincarnation. The book hadn't converted me to this philosophy, but I was intrigued enough to look for other books written by Chopra. I found that Chopra had written many books, but I chose to read *The Spontaneous Fulfillment of Desire: Harnessing the Infinite Power of Coincidence*. It was divided into two sections. The first talked about how fortunate coincidences are not random events but are actually planned and made. Who sets up these coincidences? Chopra says that a "non-local infinite intelligence" performs this task. *Hmm, sounds like a deity to me*, I thought. The second half of the book talked about the practice of meditation and its benefits. Besides improving your physical and mental health, ol' Chopra was selling the idea that continued meditation would lead to a higher incidence of lucky coincidences.

I wasn't even close to buying the premise that meditation could increase my share of lucky coincidences, but I did find another potentially good reason to practice it. I read online that some people were able to achieve out-of-body experiences through meditation, described as being able to levitate without your body to the point that you can actually look down upon it. Practitioners described a strange sensation of feeling very cold after they returned to their bodies and claimed that the body loses heat when the soul/consciousness leaves it. This idea made me consider practicing meditation for the first time. I thought that if I could personally achieve an out-of-body experience, this would prove that consciousness can indeed leave the body and still survive. Having an out-of-body experience would leave the door open to immortality. That was something certainly worth pursuing! I then decided that I was going to meditate. Did I believe that I would be able to achieve an out-of-body experience? No, but it was worth a try. I decided to make a concentrated effort for four months to see what would happen.

# Chapter 4: Opening the Door through Meditation

*Meditation is the tongue of the soul and the language of our spirit.*
—Jeremy Taylor

## Reincarnation highway mile marker: Germany, 1944

Deepak Chopra writes that to expand your spirituality, you need to meditate. He does not tell what actually happens to you when you enter that altered state; not many writers do. I guessed I would have to find out for myself. One day in January 2009, I arbitrarily decided, "Today is the day!" *Ahh, but exactly how do you do it?* I wondered. If meditation were my wife's goal, she would take a class on it. Did I do it that way? Heck, no! I just dove into it. The only guiding principle I used was that meditation is achieved by clearing your mind of all thought—a task that is easier said than done, but I was up for the challenge.

Later that night, I darkened the great room downstairs and sat on the floor with my legs crossed. Everyone else was in bed, so I knew that I would not be disturbed. Mentally only, I began to chant the chorus from George Harrison's "My Sweet Lord"—you know, the part that goes, "My sweet Lord, Hare, Hare, Krishna, Krishna"? (Hey, why not? It was the only chant I knew.) It seemed to be somewhat effective, but random thoughts still stubbornly popped into my mind. It was aggravating; when I tried not to think about something, of course, it popped right up. Everyone confronts this problem when they first try meditation, and many people are unable to overcome this obstacle. How did I overcome it? Why, with the direct, forceful way, of course! Every time a stray thought popped up, I would order it to leave by forcefully thinking, *Out!* And, surprisingly, that stray thought would stop and go away. It would then be replaced by another stray thought on a different subject, but as each new thought popped up, I ordered it away with a new *out* command. Within a short period of time, the random thoughts came slower and eventually stopped. They stopped! Nothing but quiet blackness existed inside my skull.

In my twenties, I had taught myself to get into a hypnotic state. Once in that state, my eyes would roll backward and feel heavy. With my first meditation, I was falling into the same type of feeling. My closed eyes were rolling backward. I was sinking deeper. I felt some kind of energy going out through the bridge of my nose. (Later, I learned that this was my third-eye *chakra* opening for the very first time. I will explain at the end of the chapter what chakras are.) I was enjoying this feeling when, all of a sudden, one of the metal light cans in the ceiling above me made a loud snapping noise. It was nothing out of the ordinary; the house was cooling off in the winter night. But the sudden sound startled me, and an image of a blue spark flashed behind my eyes when I heard the snap. This little disturbance brought me out of my altered state. My eyes opened, and my momentum was lost. I knew that I was done for that session, but I would definitely be back for another try.

The next night, I tried again. This time, I moved my location to the downstairs playroom, which has no windows to the outside. It's nice and dark when the lights are out, and all I could hear was the bubbling of the fish tank, perfect for late-night meditation. I went through the same routine as I had the prior night, ordering random thoughts out of my head and mentally chanting. I started to fall into a trance-like state once again. With my eyes closed, I began to see picture like visions. The first had a background of an open first-floor area in a big office building, like where the elevator banks would be. It had beautiful, polished granite walls, and walking through one of the exits was my father, wearing slacks and a nice sweater. He was with two men I didn't know. That picture disappeared and was replaced by a silly one—quarterback Brett Favre wearing a thin hillbilly goatee on his chin. Don't ask me about this one; I don't follow Brett Favre, and the image was ridiculous. (These images were the result of my falling into a "hypnagogic" state. I will save that explanation for the end of this chapter.) That picture then disappeared and was replaced by a feeling that I had experienced in my college days when I was really drunk. It was that trashed feeling, when you can stare at a wall with no thoughts going through your head and find that wall to be immensely fascinating. From that "stoned" state of mind, I drifted to sleep while sitting up. An hour or so later, I woke up and went to bed.

Early the next morning, I decided that the previous night's meditation experience had been so fun that I would do it again that morning. (Frank had found a new toy!) I went down to my home office, sat cross-legged in my leather chair, closed my eyes, and started my meditation process. After falling into a deep meditative state, I experienced something new. I felt pressure around my head like I was wearing a very heavy hat. It did not hurt; it just felt very strange. While that was going on, my head started to roll around on its own. I could have stopped it, but I let it do its thing without interference. I was like a living bobble head doll. After a while, the head rolling stopped, and I came out of the altered state. Since I was sitting in my office chair, I was right in front of my computer, and I had to find out about this head pressure that I had experienced. I Googled "meditation pressure surrounding head," and numerous web pages were listed. Scanning through them, I saw that they were all unanimous—I had just experienced my crown chakra opening up (again, see explanation at the end of this chapter.) Further research explained that this was the body's spiritual connection to the universe, and what was really surprising was that while I was looking at my computer screen, my crown chakra opened up on its own without my even meditating. I had been meditating for only three days and amazing things were happening already. I just wished I knew what they meant.

When you are looking for answers, the universe helps you out. I was to encounter many helpful people who would function as my guides on the reincarnation highway. My very first guide was Tony, a massage therapist who had hidden psychic talents. Tony fronted a rock band in his youth and still has his long hair, although it has grayed and is kept in a ponytail. He has a great sense of humor and is fun to joke around with. I went to him because my wife recommended that I see him to fix a shoulder problem. One day while he was working on my shoulder, I looked up at his long gray hair and said, "You look like a new-age type of guy. Do you meditate?" Tony smiled and responded, "Yes, I often go to the Buddhist temple downtown to meditate." Bingo! I knew I was in the presence of an expert. I then told Tony about my new meditation experiences and asked him what the crown chakra experience meant.

He told me that when your crown chakra opens, it is receiving information from the universe. Conversely, when your third-eye chakra opens, it is sending information to the universe. I was mentally puzzled at his explanation. It seemed beyond far-fetched to me, although something strange had indeed been happening to those areas of my head when I was mediating. Since I work with a website and computer network in my main business, my mind converted what Tony had said to a computer analogy—during meditation, my mind was like a remote computer trying to access a wireless network by sending and receiving information to a cosmic network. That sounded cool, but was something like that really happening?

I meditated again that night, and again the pressure developed at the top of my head. This was becoming a regular feature of my meditation practice. If I was really downloading data from the universe like Tony said, I figured that there must have been a lot of data and programs stuffed into my brain by this point. Too bad I was not able to run any of the apps yet.

Setting aside the mystery of what effect my chakras were having on me, I was ready to work on my goal of leaving my body during meditation. Once again, nobody gave me instructions on how to do this. I had a naive plan that I would try to squeeze my consciousness out of the top of my head the next time I entered a deep, altered state. Needless to say, no matter how hard I tried or how many times I commanded it to leave, nothing happened. Night after night, I kept trying but got no results. I was not getting discouraged because I had no idea if I could really accomplish an out-of-body experience.

About two months after I started to meditate, I had a pivotal experience during the night. The setting was my master bathroom, which is attached to my bedroom. In the bathroom is a whirlpool bathtub in which I occasionally read books. On that special night, I had meditated downstairs before going to sleep. While I was sleeping in bed, I had this dream.

I was lying prone in the bathtub reading a book, the title of which I do not remember. But in the book, I noted that a child had died and his parents were very upset. I thought in the dream, *It's okay. The parents will see the child again in the afterlife.* (Now that thought alone is amazing because I was still a card-carrying atheist.) Just as I thought that very thought about the parents, something grabbed me under my arms from behind and forced my arms to raise up like I was riding a roller coaster. I made the funniest response, exclaiming "Whee!" in the dream. Next, this unknown entity jerked me into a standing position in the bathtub. Half a second later, I was shooting straight up like a rocket. I went through the ceiling like the proverbial hot knife through butter. I passed through the plasterboard of the ceiling and into the attic, where I noticed that the wood joists were dark gray because there was no light up there. I didn't have any time to study the joists because I blasted right out through the roof. I quickly streaked to about a hundred feet over my house, directly over my bedroom. I was just floating there, stationary, and I looked down on my roof below. It was dark outside. I looked up and noticed the stars peeking through a gap in the cloud cover. They were absolutely brilliant. I had never seen the stars look more beautiful. Then I started to fall, and as I fell I noticed someone or something still in the air where I had been. The next thing I knew, I was laying on my stomach in my bed. I looked at the clock and it read 3:07 a.m. My body was absolutely chilled, and I do not normally get cold at night. I was shocked out of my mind and thought, *What the hell was that?*

Needless to say, it took a while for me to fall back asleep. I lay awake, thinking. *Did I just have an out-of-body experience, or was that just a dream? Well, let's see. Those ceiling joists sure looked realistic as I went through them, and my body was absolutely freezing. And what was that thing that was hovering over me as I fell back to earth? On the other hand, I was dreaming about being in my bathtub.* I got out of bed and went to a window to look at the sky; it was solidly overcast with no stars showing. I was confused. I could not determine if I had been dreaming or if I had really just been through an out-of-body experience? The next day, I gave the incident more thought. I realized that the bathtub dream was extraordinary beyond just the flying aspect. In all of my prior dreams, it was only me who touched objects in my dream. I don't remember ever having a dream in which I was touched.

The next time I saw Tony, I told him about my strange dream and asked him what he thought. He smiled and said that I had definitely had an out-of-body experience. I asked him why he was so confident in saying that, and he said that he had experienced it himself once. He said he had been sleeping in his lounge chair while watching a football game, and he got up to get a beer from his refrigerator. He then looked over his shoulder and was shocked to see himself sleeping in the lounge chair. He was so startled that he immediately snapped back into his body and woke up. *Wow*, I thought, *I really could have achieved my goal of having an out-of-body experience!* Later, on a springtime family vacation to Mexico, I had another such experience, but it was very short. I was sleeping late at night, transiting from a heavy sleep to a semiwaking state. In that state, I felt like I was flying in tight circles (without my body, of course) just below the ceiling. I swear I had had nothing to drink the prior evening. I woke up and just did not know what to think.

On *Mythbusters* on the Discovery Channel, two guys evaluate and test myths. At the conclusion of each study, they pronounce the myth busted, plausible, or confirmed (true). The myth I was evaluating was the one that says the soul can leave the body. If this was possible, then, by extension, little Jimmy from Louisiana's story of reincarnation could also be true, and that would mean that reincarnation is real. If I were a myth buster, I could only give the concept of an out-of-body experience a "plausible" rating because of the uncertainty of my experiences. I needed more proof and experiences, and I was going to receive both in a surprising way.

One special morning in March 2009, I meditated in my office. My head started to enthusiastically roll around, as normal. After a while, the head rolling suddenly shifted into an up-and-down motion, like I was nodding my head yes. Then it changed suddenly to moving back and forth, like I was shaking my head no, and then it changed back to the yes motion. It was like something was trying to signal me. Was I finally connected to the cosmic network, and was the network now confirming the connection? I took the opportunity to find out. I asked mentally, *Are you signaling yes and no?* My head moved in the yes response and stopped. I asked mentally, *Will you answer questions?* My head moved in the yes response and stopped again. I had no idea who I was talking to in my head, but I found this event to be the most fascinating moment of my life. Now, what would be the first yes or no question that I would ask this entity? World War II was calling me. The German Wehrmacht was calling to me. The homing beacon I described in Chapter 2 was now on and functioning. Of course, I asked, *Was I a German soldier in my prior life?* My head shook yes.

*Oh, my God!* Now there were so many more questions to ask, but how could I get information if I could only get yes or no answers? I realized that I had to prompt the entity with very detailed questions.

*When did I die? 1941?* No. *1942?* No. *1943?* No. *1944?* Yes. *Was I on the eastern front?* Yes.

I wanted to know my name, but the only way to do it was to call out individual letters. *Okay, I'll do it that way. What was my first name? A?* No. *B?* No. And on it went until *O* was awarded with a yes. Repeating this laborious process, I learned that my first name had been Otto. Moving on to my last name, the same process spelled out the name Kostermann.

*Was I an officer?* No. *Was I sniper?* No. *How did I die? Shot?* No. *Artillery strike?* No. I threw out a wild guess. *Bayoneted?* Yes.

*Oh, great,* I thought. *What a way to go.*

*What was my regiment?* Using the same process as I had with my name, I got to an answer of "Twenty-Third." *What was my division?* Eleventh. *If I wasn't an officer, was I a sergeant?* Yes. *What was my hometown?* Mand. (Here, I made the mistake of not suggesting any letters after I got the *D* because I thought I had received the complete name.)

By this time, I was so bursting with excitement that I came out of my altered state. I wrote down all of these answers on a sheet of paper so that I would not forget them, and then I dashed over to the computer to verify them. Just to see what information I could get from the Internet, I Googled the name Otto Kostermann. I did not expect any hits, and unfortunately, I was correct. I did find out that there was a Twenty-Third Regiment that belonged to the Eleventh Prussian Infantry Division. This was a direct hit as far as verification! As I had never read about this unit before, I could not have dredged this information from my subconscious. As far as trying to find Mand, Germany, I was unsuccessful. But then I remembered that a great deal of German land had been taken after the war by Poland and Russia, and if I had belonged to a Prussian division, then I had obviously once been a Prussian. Almost all Prussian towns and cities were annexed by Poland and Russia and renamed with Polish and Russian names. I then found a website that had a conversion table, showing the old German town names and the new Slavic ones. I found three towns that started with "Mand." To narrow the choices down, I used the following logic: German army divisions recruited soldiers from defined geographical regions. The Eleventh Division recruited from the areas surrounding the cities of Rastenburg and Allenstein, and only one of the three towns, Mandeln, was close to Rastenburg. As such, Mandeln would be the best candidate for my old hometown.

During my next meditation session the next morning, I asked this mysterious entity whether Mandeln was my hometown. My head shook yes. *Wow!* I then moved on to other questions. I learned that, as Otto, I had been born on May 5, 1922, and had died on the night of May 1, 1944. I was only twenty-two years old when I was killed. I learned that I had four brothers and one sister. My father's name was Dieter, my mother's name was Laura, and I had a Polish girlfriend named Lana.

When little Jimmy's dad made all of the fantastic connections of World War II to his son, his exclamation was, "You could have poured my brains right out of my ears! I just couldn't believe it!" I knew now exactly how he felt. This experience was absolutely incredible, and only by going through it personally could I possibly believe that it was real. I can honestly say that if I, at the age of forty, was reading these words written by someone else, I never would believe it. I would have thought that this past-life information had come from a subconscious mind that wanted to fulfill a fantasy about being a German soldier. Trust me, this would be no fantasy for me because I know from my years of reading that the German soldiers had absolutely miserable lives full of pain, lice, and hunger. No, thanks; I would not want any part of that if I had a choice.

In following meditation sessions, I actually pushed on beyond my life as Otto. I asked what year I had died in my life before Otto. The answer was 1918. *Uh-oh,* I thought. *That's the end of World War I.*

*Was I a German soldier also in that life?* Yes. *What was my name?* Through the spelling method, I came up with Alfred Hindiman.

*How was I killed?* Shot. *By whom?* British.

*When was Alfred born?* 1900.

It seemed that the twentieth century had not been a good century for me as I had apparently been killed in action twice. That got me to thinking, *How far do I go back?* To answer that question, I asked the following questions: *Was I on earth in the 1800s?* Yes. *1700s?* Yes. *1600s?* Yes. *1500s?* Yes. *1400s?* Yes. *1300s?* Yes. *1200s?* Yes. *1100s?* Yes. *1000s?* No. *During this time, was all of my time spent as a German?* Yes.

*My God,* I thought. *According to this mysterious source of information, I have been around for almost a thousand years! And as a German! That explains some things.* (Note: There is an inherent disadvantage in being able to ask only yes and no questions. I should have kept my questioning going through the centuries before the year 1000, but I stopped to move on to other topics. Later events would show that I lived many lives well before the year 1000.)

I asked more questions. *Who was I before Alfred?* Karl Hindiman. *Was I related to Alfred?* Yes. *Was I his grandfather?* Yes. (Wow, what a strange concept.) *What did Karl do for a living?* Dairy farmer. (Come to think of it, I have always had a deep respect for and interest in farms in my current life.)

Well, to say the least, I was staggered to learn this information. I still had no idea how this reincarnation process worked, but I was convinced that it is real. I felt elation because I had discovered a form of immortality. My consciousness is not going to die, nor will that of each of my loved ones! My "Mythbuster meter" moved from "plausible" to "confirmed," in my mind. However, I do not have any expectations that reincarnation is confirmed in your mind. You have to live through this experience before you can really believe it. Beyond believing it myself, I wanted to know more. I wanted to know how it all worked and, especially, the identity of who was giving me this information. Was it the universal intelligence that Chopra had written about, or was it something else?

My shoulder was getting better, but I still needed to see Tony for more treatment. I took the next opportunity to tell him about the past-life information that had been given to me, and I asked him who he thought was giving me this information. He told me that it was probably my spirit guides.

*Spirit guides? That sounds kind of hokey*, I thought. "What are those?" I asked.

"Well, everyone is assigned spirit guides to help them out in life," he said.

"Really? I have never heard of them," I said. *What a ridiculous idea*, I thought.

Tony then told me that he had noticed that the same spirit was always with me when I came to see him.

"Who is he, and what does he look like?" I asked.

"I don't know," he replied. "These spirits look like shadows to me when I see them out of the corner of my eye. I don't pay attention to them."

I needed more guidance on how to travel in this new world that I had found, but where would I find someone who knew about this strange Twilight Zone world? Once again, ask and the universe will provide in surprising ways.

My wife, Karol, has had a good friend named Linda since her first marriage. Linda is a professional human resources consultant who gave Karol and me our first consulting account. After I got to know her, Linda became a wise mentor to me, especially in the areas of human relations and personality types. I was still trying to get my head around the past-life information that had been given to me. I had no idea whether Linda practiced meditation, but something within me told me I should talk to her. I called and asked her if she meditated. "Why, yes, I do," she said. I then told her about my meditation experiences and the information that had been given to me. Instead of being incredulous, Linda was delighted. She told me that I was making fantastic progress considering the amount of time that I had put into my meditation practice. She then stunned me when she told me that she was a certified psychic. When I expressed my surprise that I had never known that, she said that she keeps that fact very low-key. She then told me about her past lives, one of which she had lived as a deaf French girl. This experience led her to become a speech therapist in her current life when she first got out of college. She strongly warned me to be careful about whom I communicated with "on the other side." She said that there are malicious spirits out there who lead people astray. She then proceeded to explain that she could both hear and see spirits, which is defined as being clairaudient and clairvoyant. Since I did not have these capabilities but had received information through head motion, she categorized me as a clairsentient psychic.

"What does that exactly mean?" I asked.

"That means that you are a person who receives psychic information physically," she said.

*Oh, my God!* I thought. *Me—a psychic? No way!* It's not that I didn't want to be a psychic; I just did not believe in such things. What is the old saying? "You can lead a horse to water, but you can't make him drink." While I wasn't ready to accept the idea that I was a psychic, Linda did me the service of pointing me in the right direction. She confirmed her own reincarnation experiences, which showed me that I was not alone. Were there even more people like me out there?

Earlier in this chapter, I used the terms *chakras* and *hypnagogic states*. I discovered the background of these phenomena much later in my journey, but I believe it would be beneficial to share it with you at this point.

We have already defined your consciousness or your soul as a form of energy. This energy force resides throughout your body at a subatomic level. Energy forces such as electricity and magnetism are surrounded by energy waves. According to Eastern religious thought, the soul as an energy force displays its energy waves in seven parts of the body known as chakras. Each chakra has its own function. By opening up the crown and third-eye chakras in my head through meditation, I was able to make a connection to the universal consciousness that Chopra wrote about, and that connection allowed information about my past lives to become available to me. To access this information, my brain had to be tuned like a radio to receive the frequency that the universe broadcasts on. Normally waking brain waves are too low to pick up the universe's frequency. To reach it, your brain waves must go up to the frequency commonly achieved during your deepest dreamless sleep, known as delta waves. The act of meditation allows your brain to progress from the "awake" beta brain waves to alpha waves, theta waves, and finally the delta waves while still remaining awake. Theta waves are where dreams occur. When I saw those strange pictures during meditation, my brain was sinking from the alpha wave stage and passing quickly through the theta wave region. It was at this stage that the pictures flashed and then disappeared as I left the theta stage and went to the delta stage. This brief stay at the theta phase is called being in a hypnagogic state. Tony has always dismissed the images at the theta stage as distractions, but I have always thought they were cool and enjoyed them.

# Chapter 5: Finding Other Members of the Club

*Being at a club that supported me meant a lot.* —David Beckham

## Reincarnation highway mile marker: USA, 2009

I had stumbled upon a strange new world all by myself, but I had no one to really share it with. Karol was interested in hearing about my adventures, but she kept the whole thing at arm's length because it was just too "out there" for her. After I had encouraged her to try to meditate, she tried it alone just once at night after the kids went to sleep. I helped her get started and then left the bedroom. When I came back later, she was laying prostrate on the floor chanting, "Let it go. Let it go." She had definitely gone into a deep trance. I was excited that she was able to achieve that the first time she tried it and thought I might have gained a meditation partner that night, but when she came out of it, she declared that she did not want to go back there. Back to square one. My interest in group meditation was piqued when I read on the Internet that a group setting can intensify the meditation experience. So in the early summer of 2009, I went on a search to find a meditation group.

I first thought that I could use my friend Nooresh as a resource. Nooresh is a friendly, middle-aged Indian man whom I met at the park across the street from my house. One day I went up to him and asked, "Hey, Nooresh, you meditate, don't you?" He got a sheepish look on his face like a Catholic who had to admit that he had not been going to confession. "Not as much as I should," he answered. I told him about my meditation experiences and that I had uncovered my past lives. He was amazed and exclaimed enviously, "I never got that far!" I then asked him if he knew of any local meditation groups, and he promised me that he would check around and asked for my phone number. A couple of days later, an Indian gentleman called and told me that Nooresh had referred him to me. He invited me to attend a local Hindu temple on Sunday morning for a meditation meeting. I eagerly accepted and went the next Sunday morning. Unfortunately, it wasn't really a meditation group but the equivalent of a Hindu Sunday school session. It was interesting but was not for me. That very same Sunday, I left with my family to drive up to Niagara Falls for a little vacation.

At the Niagara Falls Visitors Center on the Canadian side, Karol and the kids wanted to visit a souvenir shop in the building. I don't like souvenir shops, so I stayed in the lobby just to watch the crowd. There, I noticed a Buddhist monk sitting alone on a bench. He was an older man with a shaven, bald head and was wearing colorful robes. I approached him, said hello, and asked him if I could sit with him. He smiled and said yes. I told him that I had found past lives when I meditated and asked him what it meant.

He calmly replied, "They are only past lives. They mean nothing."

I responded, "They mean something to me because I died violently in wars."

"Don't worry," he said. "It's all but a dream."

I had no idea what he was talking about, but I did not press for an explanation because I knew it would be a long and deep conversation. (Eventually, I would come to learn what he was saying. The answer is, as I suspected, really deep and is touched upon in Appendix 2.) After talking a bit more, I thanked him for his time and wisdom and went back to my family.

When I got home from Niagara Falls, I wanted to find a meditation group more than ever. I just had to find other people who were experiencing what I was experiencing. I Googled "meditation groups Powell Ohio." The results referred me to a very useful website called MeetUp.com, which allows you to find groups that align with your interests. Luckily, there was a meditation group that met every Tuesday night in a nearby community. I signed up and notified them that I would attend the next session.

The Tuesday night meeting was at the home of a woman named Brenda Posani. Brenda is a very vivacious, bubbly, red-haired woman in her forties. She grew up in the hills of Kentucky and still has a bit of the Kentucky twang and mannerisms. I knocked on her door and was led to a lower-level family room where twelve to fourteen people were sitting in circle of chairs. Brenda called the group to order. As the meditation group's name was A Greater Love, she led a short talk about love among the members of the group and then began conducting my long-awaited group meditation session. She used a strange-sounding recording on a CD that was a combination of synthesized music and a heartbeat to put the listener in a deeper trance. I must say that it worked fairly well because I did go into a deeper-than-average altered state. When she guided us all out of the meditation, she then announced that it was time for psychic training. (*What? I thought this was a meditation group!*) Brenda saw the confusion on my face and told me that this was, indeed, a psychic class.

"But I'm not a psychic," I said, forgetting that Linda had already identified me as one.

"Anybody can be one," she replied. "All it takes is practice. Give it a try."

*What the heck. It can't hurt anything, but this is stupid,* I thought. So I dubiously went along with it.

Brenda split us into pairs. My partner was a friendly, middle-aged blonde named Cheryl. As I sat next to her, I could—honest to God—feel an energy force around her. This energy is best described as similar to that surrounding two magnets of the same polarity when you try to put them together. You feel the magnetic force pushing each magnet away from the other. It was like my head was one of those magnets, feeling a magnetic force pushing against it. The exercise was to try to figure out what was going on in your exercise partner's house. Brenda explained to me that the polite way of intruding on someone else's mind is to first ask, "Can I step into your vibration?" So my partner and I both asked and received our mutual permission to invade each other's minds. *So how do I do this?* I thought. *Well, why not ask the mysterious source that I talk to in my meditations to help?* So I went into a light meditation and started to interrogate my mysterious source.

*Does this woman have children?* Yes. *Anything going on with her children?* Yes. *What is going on?* Job. *Is a child going to get a job soon?* No. *Is the child interviewing?* No. *Does the child know what he or she wants to do?* No. *By the way, the child in question—a daughter?* No. *A son?* Yes. *Is that what I'm supposed to find out, that the son cannot make up his mind about what to do?* Yes.

Well, surprisingly enough, I had come up with some kind of answer, but was it correct? The time came to reveal everyone's readings in front of the group. Cheryl went first and actually provided an accurate description of something that had gone on in my home. My memory of what her reading was is lost to me because I never wrote it down. (I never expected that I would be writing a book about these experiences.) I did not store Cheryl's reading of me in my memory because it was drowned out by the astonishing results of the reading that I had performed on Cheryl. I asked her if she had a son, and she said yes. I asked if he was looking for a job, and she said yes. I then asked her if he could not make up his mind about what he wanted to do, and she again said yes. "Is this the current issue at your house?" I asked. She again said yes. I was absolutely amazed that I had pulled this information literally out of my ear! Brenda was just beaming at me. She had a new student.

What happened next was even more astounding. During a break in our "instructional class," Brenda pulled me aside and told me a very personal secret that is known only to my wife and me. I was absolutely stunned that she could know this. It was not embarrassing, only deeply personal. I had given Brenda permission to step into my vibration, and I guess my "vibration" was emanating that information. She obviously did it as a demonstration of her capabilities. She assured me that she does not share these things with other people and that she would soon forget it. With that personal demonstration, I was a complete believer in her powers.

Let me make some comments about this group of psychics. Everyone there had different levels of talent and ability, ranging from almost no ability to very gifted. But this particular group of people shared a common trait that I found surprising—no one there was doing anywhere above average economically. You would think that people with psychic powers would be doing pretty well in life. I mean, after all, if you could read minds and sometimes see the future, those abilities should give you a decided advantage in life. Instead, there were some divorced moms who were experiencing financial problems. Others were between jobs or underemployed. There is nothing wrong with that—I have experienced unemployment in my own life—but the level of middle-class economic problems in the room was higher than average. I came to the realization that I was the only person in the room who had a high income. I was surprised that I was the only one. Later in my journey, I would meet some psychics who held very professional positions and were at the high end of the economic range. I guess that what I learned is that the gift of psychic ability cuts across all social levels, genders, races, and sexual orientations. The existence of psychic ability had no correlation with economic success, which meant that these people could not or would not use the power for personal gain. Which is it—could not or would not? I would need more experience in this world to learn the answer.

Earlier, I mentioned the different abilities of psychics. Let me further explain them, but I will leave out the most amazing ability (to me, at least) for the next chapter. Psychics receive messages from spiritual entities from beyond the veil. Wait a minute! Stop the presses! Did I just say *spiritual entities*? That's a big step for an atheist. I got this term from Brenda when I asked her who exactly was giving us this psychic information. Her answer was, "Angels and spirit guides, of course, and Spirit himself."

"Who is that?" I asked.

"Why, God, of course," she replied.

Remember in Chapter 1 when I said that I would absolutely believe in God if he communicated directly with me? Well, my supernatural experiences were coming very close to this, and as such, my atheism was crumbling. But that is a diversion—let me get back to describing the powers of psychics.

Psychics can receive messages from spiritual entities in one or any combination of the below methods:

- Clairvoyance—The gift of having an additional viewing screen behind your eyes on which you see pictures and moving images of things sent to you from spiritual entities just like the one I talk to in my meditations.
- Clairaudience—The gift of hearing spoken messages from spiritual entities.
- Clairsentient—The gift of feeling messages from spiritual entities. Many times this ability is not a good gift because pain can be transmitted. For example, I have seen an entity communicate the idea of a miscarriage to a female psychic, and the psychic grabbed her abdomen in pain. I have also

read of entities' transmitting chest pains when they are communicating the concept of a heart attack.

What psychic ability did I possess at this point in my spiritual journey? I was a weak clairsentient. I was not sensitive enough to pick up pain feelings (thank God!), but I could pick up yes and no answers to questions I asked. Just call me Frank, the human Ouija board. And that was the frustrating thing about being in psychic class with limited abilities. Brenda would have each of us stand up in class and give a quick reading to someone. The lucky ones, those who were clairaudient, would just have the answers quickly whispered into their brains. I had to go through the laborious process of asking, "A? B? C?" and so on to get an answer. Then the spirits changed the game on me; they stopped spelling complete words and began just giving me one letter to represent a word. So not only did I have to go through the A-B-C process, I also had to play the equivalent of *Wheel of Fortune* with no vowels to get my answer. Needless to say, it took me a long time to complete a reading. I would jokingly chastise the other group members that they were connected to the high-speed "psychic internet" while I was still using the old dial-up version. Brenda assured me that with further meditation and practice that I would soon have all the abilities that everyone had. (That sounded good to me!)

There remains one more thing to relate about Brenda's teachings that summer. At the end of each psychic class, she would go to each of us and give us a short reading. One of her readings in August told me that the spirits were going to "spoon feed" me information over time. Looking back at this, what they were saying was that they were going to release information to me slowly over my journey. I found that even if I asked for specific information about a past life or other information, they would give it to me only by their schedule, not mine. There seemed to be some kind of plan in place. You will see this slow release of information play out over the rest of the book, and it was frustrating at times when I had to wait for things to be revealed.

That same summer, an unconventional psychic provided a hint as to which roads my spiritual journey would take me on from that point. I had to go back to Tony for more treatment of my shoulders, and during one session, he told me that I had an "energy" cyst in my left shoulder.

"What's an energy cyst?" I asked.

He said that the body can retain the imprints of physical trauma in the tissues. These energy imprints can also include the intense feelings that occurred at the time of injury. He was probing my shoulder with his eyes closed while he explained. He then asked, "You said you were stabbed in your past life as a soldier?" I said yes. He then said that he sensed the image of a large knife stuck in my shoulder where the energy cyst was.

"You mean energy cysts can come from prior lives?" I asked incredulously.

"Absolutely," he said. He then told me that he was going to eliminate this cyst. He closed his eyes tightly and concentrated with both hands on my left shoulder. After about a minute, he exclaimed, "Ouch! That was a nasty one!" He then explained that this ball of energy had jumped from my shoulder, gone into his arm, and then traveled down his body to where his foot was touching the floor. It had then exited his body through his foot. He told me that he could actually feel it move through his body and that it was not pleasant at all. He also said that I had a smaller one on the right side of my body below the rib cage and proceeded to work on that one.

"How many of these things do I have?" I asked.

"Let's just say that the bayonet was not the only time you were wounded," he answered. "You have wounds all over your body."

# Chapter 6: Reunion with My Father

*Every parting gives a foretaste of death, every reunion a hint of the resurrection.*

—Arthur Schopenhauer

## Reincarnation highway mile marker: USA, 2009

After each psychic training session, Brenda would host a little social event in her kitchen. During one of these, I overheard her telling a story of doing a reading in which she connected a client to her dead parent. Brenda was speaking as if it was no big deal, but I was amazed. I asked her if she could do that for me, and she said, "Absolutely." I immediately thought about how great it would be to talk to my dad again. Did I believe that Brenda could really do this? Not really, but it was well worth a try. Without hesitation, I made an appointment with her to try to communicate with my lost father.

I should have marked down the date; I never knew that I would be writing a book. Anyway, it was sometime in late September 2009 that I went to Brenda's house on a cloudy afternoon to try to make contact with my dad. After letting me into the house, Brenda guided me to her living room, where she sat on her couch, and I settled into a comfortable chair opposite her. I remember that she did not turn on any lights, and so it was a little bit dark. I was to learn in the future about the usual process that Brenda goes through when she makes contact with the spirits of the departed. It is designed to get some psychic insight into the person that she is doing the reading for. It's a fascinating routine in which she draws out past events and personality traits of her client. She did state some interesting and accurate things about me personally, but I did not write them down or remember them because of what happened next. Brenda was sort of slouching back in her couch when she said, "Oh, my! What an entrance! Your dad just came in the room projecting a very big, strong appearance. He is now sitting here with his legs crossed like this." She crossed her legs in that unusual manner that my dad did. "He keeps saying to you, 'Good job. Good job.'"

That phrase was one of the last things he said to me when he was on his deathbed in Jacksonville. Brenda then said that my dad kept repeating that he was sorry, "so sorry." Tears welled up in my eyes because I knew that he was referring to a big battle between my mother and me and all the many times that he took my mother's side. Out loud, I told him that he had nothing to be sorry for now and that it was all right. Through Brenda, my dad then revealed, "I want you to know that, in life, I put on a very confident face. In truth, though, I was unconfident and many times unsure of myself. I regret that I put too much emphasis on material things. These things really are unimportant. I should have been putting more emphasis on relationships. Relationships cannot be bought." He then said something that will be addressed in a future chapter—"I now know that you had difficult times in your teen years."

To change the mood and get on to happier subjects, I asked Brenda to ask my dad if he was responsible for the recent outbreak of chauvinism that my son, Brian, had been exhibiting. Brenda smiled as she silently listened to the response. She said that my dad laughed and said, "Why are you blaming me for this? This is all your fault!"

I then changed my method of communication. Instead of addressing my questions to Brenda, I just said them out loud to the living room. "Hey, Dad, would you believe I was a German soldier in World War II?" Brenda responded on behalf of my dad, "I don't have to believe when I already know." The response puzzled me, and it showed on my face. I had never heard my dad say that phrase before, but I knew that it sounded like something he would say, if that makes sense. Brenda saw my puzzlement and said, "Your dad knows that you were a German soldier."

By this time, I was absolutely astounded by this experience and wanted to write down what my father was saying. I scrambled to Brenda's kitchen to grab a pen and went back to my chair in the living room.

Luckily, I had some paper in my back pocket on which I had printed an article that I wanted to share with Brenda. I started to scribble furiously on the back of the paper; this is how I was able to capture the details that I am now sharing with you.

I wanted to clear up a mystery that happened after Dad died. "Hey, Dad," I said, "was that you in the van when I saw your face on Brian?"

"Yes, that was me. I wanted you to know that I was around."

*Oh, my God,* I thought. *I wasn't imagining things. That incident was real.*

"God, you scared the crap out of me!" I said. It appeared that the scene was "played" to Brenda psychically, and she chimed in with, "That incident happened in your garage, right?" I said yes.

I asked my dad if he was doing any flying over there, and he responded, "Everyone flies over here." I said, "What do you do on the other side?"

"I spend a lot of time with you and your brother and sister. I am with you in your office. I watch you work on your computer all day." (This is true; I do have a home office, and I do spend almost all of my time on the computer.)

Now, knowing that my dad spends time with me in my house just like Concetta Bertoldi describes in her book *Do Dead People Watch Us Shower?*, I wanted to ask him about the things that were going on in my household. During the summer of 2009, Karol and I had undertaken a major kitchen remodeling, and I asked my dad what he thought about the outcome. He responded, "Too much work. It was unnecessary."

In August 2009, my family prevailed against me, and we purchased a papillon puppy. My main complaint was that when the kids were in school, I would be alone with the dog when I was trying to work in my office. I asked my dad what he thought about the dog, and Brenda received an image from my father and laughed. She said that my dad was pointing his finger to his head like a gun and was pulling the trigger.

"Your dad says that the dog is too noisy and irritating," she said. This was true. "He also says that the dog can see him and that he riles up the dog sometimes just to get him going." All of these mannerisms are consistent with those of my dad during his life.

I asked Dad what he thought about his grandchildren. He responded that Brian was kind of intense and that Jani is a princess. He said that Jani feels his presence and that she is very spiritual. He then switched subjects and told me that he was worried about my brother Dave's smoking habits. This was something he was always worried about in his life.

I then asked him if he spent any time at his house in Florida, and his response surprised me. Brenda started to pound the armrest of her sofa with the palm of her hand and responded for my dad, "Never, never, never. I don't go where I'm not wanted." I reassured him that he was very much welcome in my house. He then showed Brenda a symbol of a large tree with all of its limbs cut off, and Brenda said that this image represented my family and how it had split since my dad died. This was certainly true. Karol always prophesied that when my dad died, my family would lose its cohesion and fall apart. She was right. Dad then made an unusual comment about my mother. He said that she doesn't spend much time thinking about the future or the present but spends most of her time thinking about the past.

I asked my dad if I could communicate with him during my meditation periods, and he said that he was there but couldn't get close to me because two spirits that he did not know were dominating access to me. He told me to keep the others at bay when meditating and choose him. Brenda then told me that she sensed that a spirit named Rollo was hovering close to me during my meditations.

My father said that he was talking to his "Council of Elders" to see if they could arrange a future lifetime in which he and I would be twin brothers born in a town somewhere on the coast. My dad just loved living by the sea, and I was touched that he would want to spend another lifetime with me. Somehow, I don't think the powers in charge would arrange that. It would be too nice of a life.

To clear up another mystery, I asked him if he had stopped drinking his essiac tea to keep his cancer at bay. He laughed and said that he did know about that but that he would take the vitamins that I take in the morning that come in a green bottle with the flowers on the label. Well, it just so happens that I do take a supplement in the morning that's in a green plastic bottle with pink flowers on it. I was to learn in the future that spirits just love to make validating statements in psychic readings to certify that what they are communicating is true. The mention of my vitamin supplement bottle was this reading's validating statement. In the future, I would see validation over and over again in readings.

I'm not quite sure how the reading wound down and ended. It had to have lasted at least an hour. Afterward, I was just blown away. It was one of the most important experiences of my life.

What did I get out of the experience besides being reunited with my father? My prior life as a German soldier was confirmed by another source. I learned that a person's personality goes forward and exists after that person dies. In the case of my father, he sure did not change much other than being more "spiritual" and understanding. The concept of the Council of Elders was confirmed. (The Council of Elders is your personal oversight board of senior spirits who oversee your spiritual development.) Finally, I learned that spirits live with us and that we are completely unaware of this fact. What next? I wanted to further explore my past lives in more detail. Having discovered Brenda's powers, I knew that she was going to be my tour guide.

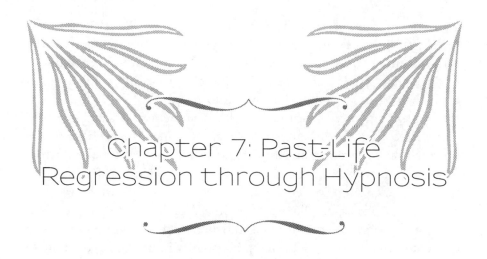

# Chapter 7: Past-Life Regression through Hypnosis

*Actually, actually, when he first put us into hypnosis, he didn't know what he was going to get.*

—Betty Hill

## Reincarnation highway mile marker: Russian Front, 1942

For those of you who remember the *X-Files* TV series from the 1990s, a particular *X-Files* episode resonates with this book. FBI agents Scully and Mulder were investigating a Jim Jones–like cult in Tennessee. Mulder had a high level of romantic interest in a particular woman in the cult, and he tried to save her. But being at the cult compound caused Agent Mulder to have flashback memories of events that had occurred there during the Civil War, only Mulder's memories were seen from the framework that he had actually lived them. To get to the bottom of these memories, Mulder went through a series of deep hypnosis sessions to uncover the story of his unexplained memories.

This type of hypnosis is real and is called past-life regression. The hypnotherapist puts the subject into such a deep trance that memories from earlier lives can be recalled. In this process, a person can remember events and places, and some hypnotherapists can even take a subject to the time period when he or she is in between lives in heaven. In Mulder's hypnosis session, it was revealed that Mulder and Scully were comrade Confederate soldiers who died in battle at that location in Tennessee and that the woman from the cult was Mulder's wife in that past life. As the therapy session progressed, it appeared that these same three souls maintained a practice of sharing other lives together. Mulder recalled being in a Jewish family with the souls of Scully and the woman from the cult in Poland during the Holocaust in WWII. Mulder was thoroughly convinced that the results of the therapy session were true and shared them with Scully, who was, of course, skeptical. Mulder then had the cult woman undergo the same hypnosis, and she confirmed Mulder's memories in her session. I remember being fascinated with this episode and the concepts it addressed. First of all, there was that reincarnation idea again, but it was set in a Western location rather than Asia, where reincarnation is an established belief. Then there was the concept of Scully's having been a male soldier in one life and a female in another. Sexy Scully used to be a gruff soldier? That's really different. Another interesting idea was the concept of particular souls spending time together in successive lives. I'm not saying that I believed any of it after watching the TV show, but I thought it was all fascinating and very thought provoking.

Unlike Mulder, I received only minimal information about being a German soldier in World War II; I did not receive memories. After I received information from my meditation, I recalled this particular *X-Files* episode, and being a curious fellow, I really wanted to know my story as Otto. Did I like being a soldier? Was I a good soldier? What did I do? Who were my friends? Did I win any medals, and if so, how did I earn them? Coincidentally, Brenda, besides being a psychic, is trained in hypnoregression.

In this book's timeline, it is the fall of 2009. Brenda had opened a store called the Mystic Nirvana. It had a new-age type gift shop in the front, and the back of the store had rooms for psychic readings. Brenda had moved both her training classes and psychic readings to the store, but there had been a two-month break in our psychic training classes because Brenda was devoting all of her time to opening the store. In this interim, I had not seen Brenda at all. When the store finally opened, I called and asked her if we could recover some memories from World War II. She said, "Sure! Let's give it a try." We set up an appointment for early afternoon on a weekday.

Because I work for myself, I have the luxury of taking off when I want. I was really looking forward to this appointment, almost as much as I had been to meeting my father again. I had this fantasy that

Brenda would be able to put me into a dream state in which I could actually see the events that I participated in. In a sense, I was hoping to achieve clairvoyance through this hypnosis process. Just before I had to leave for the appointment, I got a business-related phone call that delayed my departure. I hit the road late and had to speed to get there on time. You really hope to enter a hypnosis session in a relaxed state, but I was hyped up from speeding through traffic—not a good start. Brenda greeted me and led me to her office, where she told me to get comfortable on a couch. She darkened the lights and then went through her warm-up routine, just like she had before giving a psychic reading. It was then that she gave me some really astounding information. She said that they (the other side) were telling her that I had been very religious in many of my past lives. In fact, I had been a priest many times. She said, "I see a vision of you as a Mayan priest, and you were pretty hard core about it."

"That would be me," I said. Though I had limited knowledge of Mayan history, I did know that that region and time was known for gory ritual human sacrifice. "I sure hope that I wasn't one of those guys who cut out human hearts!" I exclaimed. Brenda shrugged her shoulders and said, "Sometimes you're the persecutor, and sometimes you're the persecuted." *Wonderful*, I thought. *That's reassuring.*

Brenda then said that I had been a Catholic priest a couple of times. For some reason, the memory of my first girlfriend's parents' shunning me for not being Catholic came to my mind, and the cosmic irony of it all made me laugh inside. Brenda received another vision and said, "In medieval times, you were pretty high up in the Catholic hierarchy!"

*That would mean archbishop or cardinal*, I thought. *Frank, the atheist, a cardinal? No way!* "But I have been an atheist all my life," I said. "How can that be?"

"Are you an atheist now?" she asked.

*Well, that's a good question*, I thought. With all of this exposure to the supernatural, I wasn't an atheist anymore. But I didn't know what I was at the moment.

With that, Brenda suggested that we move on to the hypnosis. I was still reeling from the exposure of my religious past, but I moved on. Brenda started to play the CD that she used in our meditation group and then went through the pretty typical routine that hypnotists use to put people under. Since I was still hyped up from driving fast to the appointment, it took a while for me to slip into another state and I had trouble getting into a very deep state. I don't remember exactly how she got me to talk about it, but I described a battle scene in Northern Russia that had occurred during my life as Otto. Brenda asked me to look at my reflection in a pool of water and describe what I saw. Well, since I'm not clairvoyant, I can't see anything in my mind's eye, but I described what I thought I'd see. I told her that my boots were black and dirty and my pants were gray and also dirty. I was wearing a gray helmet, and I had short brown hair. I was about five foot eleven and had brown stubble on my face. It was October. There were ten of us in a rolling tundra–like field. It was very desolate, and there was light, patchy snow on the ground. I was leading a group of young soldiers, some of whom were only eighteen years old. Gunther and Hans were with me. They followed me and trusted me. I really didn't want to be there. I didn't believe that we should be there. It was the Nazi swine government officials who sent us there, and now we were stuck in this do-or-die situation because of them. Up ahead on a desolate slope was a log barricade, and the Russians were behind it. They started firing their machine guns. Well, we were in the shit again. My group was pinned down, but we spread out and started crawling toward the Russians' position. One of us got close enough to throw a "potato masher" grenade toward them, and we killed all of the Russians there.

Brenda then said, "You were pretty young to have all of this responsibility. Look on the ground. What do you see?"

"I see dead Russians. They were not regular soldiers and not very good."

"Do you feel guilty?" asked Brenda.

I answered in German, "No, I do not." Then I switched back to English. "They were trying to kill us. It's them or us. I am well past being sorry. No time for guilt because I am sure that my time is coming soon anyway."

Brenda then directed me to tell her about when I died.

"The captain made us go on a night patrol to scout out an area. I do not like the idea, but I go anyway. What choice do I have? I am wearing a green uniform parka, and it is chilly. I am twenty-two and lead two other men on this patrol. We get into some kind of trouble, and we sneak into a house to try to escape. We go through an open door, but there are Russians inside. There's a struggle in the dark, and I get stabbed in the left chest. I try to get out, but that's it. I'm done."

What was I experiencing during this process? Not much—my eyes were closed. I didn't see anything except a curious cross (not a crucifix) shape behind my eyes that spun slowly and continuously. I had never seen that image before this reading.

Let's analyze this experience. Did my hypnosis story contain actual memories, or were they just personal fantasies derived from war stories that I have read? At that point, I really had no idea. But Brenda extracted from me new details in the story. The death scene in the house at night was new, and the desolate slope represents a thought or a feeling that seems familiar, something just out of my memory's reach. This story could actually be true; I would just need more corroborating information to confirm it. Regardless, a new focus for my curiosity had come on the scene—the revelation that I used to be a high-level Catholic cleric. That idea alone was fascinating, but high-level clerics actually have information recorded about them, which would be able to confirm the revelations that were being given to me. I was starting to get the idea that my little ride down the reincarnation highway was going to involve more than learning about the life of Otto Kostermann.

# Chapter 8: A Spirit Gives New Road Directions

*Ghosts, like ladies, never speak till spoken to.*

—Richard Harris Barham

## Reincarnation highway mile marker: Medieval Europe

My wife, Karol, is many things—a force of nature, a great mother, and one of the best business managers I have ever seen. She is like Miss Ellen (Scarlett O'Hara's mother in *Gone with the Wind*); she runs the plantation, and it revolves around her. In my family, she is the sun in the center of our family solar system, and I am a pesky comet with an irregular orbit, disrupting her natural order of things. Karol is also a big extrovert. Extroverts live to be with groups of people. Take them away from social groups, and they will wither away and die. However, members of groups must adhere to "group think" and common conventions. If you stray too far from the common conventions of the group, you will be excluded. As such, Karol is very reluctant to be perceived as being unconventional because she will lose her treasured access to social groups. I, however, am definitely unconventional, and I really do not care what other people think. I do care about other people, but if they do not accept me for who I am, it's no loss to me. It *is* a loss to Karol, though, so she expends a lot of effort trying to keep my unusual ways out of public view—things like my machine-gun collection and the fact that, as a fifty-five-year-old, I slap on my German helmet and take on all the neighborhood teenage boys in airsoft wars. (You ought to see me—I am a German Rambo taking on all these kids in the woods and setting them to flight.) Anyway, imagine what it was like for her when I entered the psychic world. She would say, "That's great, sweetie, but let's not tell the neighbors or the parents at school, okay?" To her credit, she was always interested in my stories and what I found, but she did not want to dive too deeply into analyzing my experiences with me. She definitely maintained a distance from my new world. It was a little too creepy or scary for her taste, and she just was not ready to think about the issues it brought up.

When I returned home from my reunion with my father at Brenda's home, I told Karol about the whole experience. She was fascinated with the story and asked a few skeptical questions to ensure that Brenda did not get this information from other sources or from me. I assured her that the experience was completely legitimate. But what made her jaw literally drop was my dad's reference to the green plastic vitamin bottle with pink flowers on it. I went into my closet, retrieved that vitamin bottle, and showed it to her. That validation convinced her that my experience had been real. I told her that I wanted her to have her own experience and asked her if she would be willing to go to her own reading. I really did not think that she would go for it, but she surprised me by saying yes. I am glad that she did; not only would she get a message from the spirits, but this experience would also give me clues as to where my next stop on the reincarnation highway would be.

Sometime in October 2009, I made an appointment for Karol with Brenda. Karol's only condition was that this would be her experience alone and that I could not be in the room. I drove Karol to the Mystic Nirvana and introduced her for the first time to Brenda, who warmly greeted her and led her to one of the small reading rooms. I was sitting in the larger room just outside the room that Karol was in, and the door to the reading room was paper thin; I could hear everything that was going on. The large room that I was in had a vibe. You have to be attuned to it, but strong energy waves flowed back and forth in that room. If you meditated there (and that was so easy to do there), your head would literally move and sway with the waves in that room. I don't know if it was psychic energy or spirits or both, but I always enjoyed the vibrations in that room. So while Karol was having her reading, I was comfortably bobbing away in the "psychic lake" next door, listening in.

I heard Brenda go through her standard warm-up routine, tuning into Karol's past. Brenda asked Karol if she had been in an almost-fatal car accident, and Karol responded yes. Brenda said she had visions of Karol being alone and losing control of her car on a highway, and she said that if Karol hadn't grabbed the wheel when she did, she would have died in that accident. Brenda then started to talk about our three children and their attributes. After that, spirits started to visit with Karol. Brenda told Karol that an elderly woman had come into the room and told her that she was proud of her and that she was a good mother. I don't remember the details, but Karol was able to identify this spirit as Grandma Miller, her paternal grandmother. I had coached Karol previously, telling her to ask Brenda who Karol's spirit guide was. When she did, a new spirit entered the room and identified herself as Maria. Maria told Karol that she had been her guide for a long time and that they had actually spent a life together as Gypsy sisters in medieval times. Brenda laughed when she relayed a comment from Maria, saying, "And we were not hags like the other ones!"

While this was going on, something strange was happening with me. I was in deep meditation but still listening in on Karol's reading. I was sitting straight up in a comfortable chair. On their own, my hands moved into a prayer position, and my head bowed. I had the feeling of being a priest in deep prayer at an altar. I just went with the feeling and did not fight it, remaining in that prayer position. Next, by their own volition, my hands separated, and my right hand moved into a benediction gesture as shown below:

Once again, I just went with it. I didn't know much about the gesture, but I did remember seeing photos of popes and bishops using it to bless congregations. Then, Brenda's husband, Tom, passed through the room, and my right hand dropped down into to my lap. When Tom left, it reassumed the benediction gesture. I'd never before made that gesture in my life. Someone was trying to tell me something, but I did not understand the message yet.

While I was doing my Catholic priest imitation in the next room, Karol's psychic reading was continuing. A new spirit had entered the room. Brenda said she had visions of a man somewhat obscured by cigarette smoke and with a heart operation scar on his chest. She also said that he had sandy brown hair and mentioned something about an illness associated with his head. Karol said that was her uncle Don, who had been very close to Karol when she was a child. He was a successful businessman in the 1960s who smoked heavily. He would later have a heart attack and a stroke. Karol's uncle passed the message that he was very proud of her, and then he made a validation statement that was very similar to the one my dad had said to me. This validation statement was the question, "Why did you take down those nice drapes with the blue velvet in them?" I wish I had been in the room to see Karol's reaction. It just so happened that we had been remodeling the large window in our upstairs great room. The new window configuration was a different shape than the prior windows and much bigger. As such, the prior drapes no longer fit the window and had just recently been taken down for good. Those drapes were fairly new and had blue velvet patterns. I guess Uncle Don had really liked those drapes. It wasn't my idea to take them down!

The reading pretty much wound down after that. I snapped out of my meditations as Brenda and Karol came out of the room. Karol was smiling, and I could tell she had enjoyed the experience, although she did say later that it was overwhelming. Driving on the way home, I remembered a Carlos Santana song from the seventies, and I started to sing it to Karol badly: "She was my Gypsy woman, my Gypsy woman." Karol smiled and rewarded me with a punch in the shoulder.

I then told Karol about my body's being taken over and put into prayer and benediction postures. She was incredulous and dismissed the event as something my subconscious was responsible for. I knew better because I had experienced it. I thought of those computer programs that allow you to connect to your work computer from your home computer. They allow you to have full remote control, with which you can manipulate the cursor on the distant computer's screen. That's what happened to my body in that room. Some spirit was controlling my arms to give me some kind of message. The only connection I could make was linking the benediction gesture to Brenda's prior revelation that I had once been a high-ranking member of the Catholic clergy. My final interpretation was that I was receiving a not-so-subtle nudge to explore the reincarnation highway for my Catholic clergy past.

# Chapter 9: Chief Shem

*Our first teacher is our own heart.* — Cheyenne

## Reincarnation highway mile marker: USA, 2010

My spiritual journey up to this point did not consist strictly of psychic readings; I also read a number of spiritual books. They were not Christian spiritual books, but rather books written by psychics, telling of their experiences with the other side. I also read a series of three books by Michael Newton, PhD, that addressed the use of hypnoregression to uncover people's lives in heaven that occurred between their lives on earth. The book gave a glimpse of what society is like on the other side and what people actually do there. Another series of books, called *Your Soul's Plan* by Robert Schwartz, revealed that we plan our lives before we come down to earth and live them. These authors used psychic readings to uncover how and why the subjects in the books planned their lives as they did. *Your Soul's Plan* asserted that we pick our lives, our parents, and our spouses before we come here. These assertions are admittedly radical, but they do make sense once you read the books. I felt that it would be very helpful if I could just communicate more directly with someone on the other side to determine whether what these books said was true. Up to this point in my story, I have had to use other psychics to have actual conversations with those on the other side. Instead of being restricted to using intermediaries, I wanted to hear the words from the other side with my own ears. This would allow me to pose a series of questions for myself.

I was fortunate to be able to stumble onto such an opportunity at the Mystic Nirvana. On Sunday nights, Brenda hosted a new-age church service at her store. I went every chance I got because I found that I could almost count on something memorable occurring. At a minimum, I could get a short reading from Brenda. One Sunday night, Brenda announced that we were going to have a special event. She explained that a member of our group, named Greg, was going to channel a Native American chief named Shem. (Channeling involves the spirit or ghost of a deceased person entering the body of a living person and then speaking through that living person.) Brenda said that Shem was finished reincarnating on earth and now serves as a spiritual guide. She also explained that Shem had previously channeled through Greg's mother until her death, and then Shem switched to Greg as his earthly medium. After her opening remarks, Brenda turned the meeting over to Greg and his family.

I watched from my seat in the audience of about twenty people with great interest. Greg's wife and two teenage children sat in the front row of the meeting room and were setting up a small video camera. It was explained that Greg would have no memory of this event and that it was being videotaped so that he could see what happened. Greg's family appeared quite familiar with Shem's "appearances," and I could tell that this was nothing new to them. Greg sat in the front with his eyes closed, quietly meditating. Before he got into his channeling state, he warned us that his demeanor and voice would change in this process and that he would not be aware of what was going to happen. He then closed his eyes and sunk into a meditative state while we sat quietly waiting for something to happen. The small video camera was turned on, and its red light glowed in the semidarkened room. After a little while, Greg's body kind of stiffened in his chair, and his eyes fluttered open. It was like he had just awoken from a deep sleep. He turned slightly toward the video camera and exclaimed in a voice just like the character Tonto (from *The Lone Ranger*), "Red light on again. I always see." He then looked at the small audience in front of him and said, "Many people here," and he grunted, again just like Tonto. I was transfixed watching this scene. The facial transformation in Greg was amazing. Was this real or some joke? I could not tell. There was dead air as no one knew what to say; I guess Shem wasn't prepared to give a presentation. I asked Greg's wife it was okay to ask Shem questions, and she responded yes. Here was my opportunity to ask detailed questions to a spirit about how the "other side" works, especially since Shem was supposed to be of the higher "guide" level.

My first question concerned the contradiction that if souls plan their lives before being born, how would that process permit evil acts to occur in that life? In a sense, I was seeking to learn how evil people were viewed by the spirits. I received a surprising answer.

"Are evil people and their acts planned on the other side or on this side of life?" I asked. Shem replied, "An evil person does not see his acts as evil; it is where he wants to experience growth that will determine how he will act in a life." My interpretation of his response is that a soul actually chooses to perform evil acts if they aid in his growth as a soul. His answer certainly did not support the Christian view that evil acts are punished in the afterlife.

My second question addressed planned lives again. "Is your spouse chosen for you before you come into this life?" I asked. Shem responded, "They (the wives) like to think so. You make the choice of your spouse there." With that, Shem had just confirmed the assertions in *Your Soul's Plan*.

My third question attempted to address the mystery of why my prior bloody, warrior lives were being revealed to me in this life. I asked, "What good do my warrior memories from past lives do me in this life?" Shem answered, "Do you not provide for your family and protect them in this life?" *Is he suggesting that the aggressiveness of a warrior echoes into my current life?* I wondered. The pursuit of this answer would obviously require more investigation. In retrospect, I should have followed up with a more specific question, but I not had time to prepare for this opportunity. I switched to another subject.

My fourth question was an attempt to see just how far back Shem's soul went as a Native American. "Did you live at the time when the great ice sheets covered this land?" "No," he replied. Then I wanted to find out how recently Shem had lived on earth, so I asked, "Were you living when the white man came?" Shem said, "Why do you ask that question?" I replied that I was an amateur historian and was curious, but Shem said, "I do not want to talk about those things here. I want to talk about spiritual things. There is much love in this room."

In an attempt to find out how much of a person's personality goes forward from life to life, I said, "I have noticed by talking to my dead father that much of his strong personality has stayed with him in the afterlife. Is that normal? Do you keep the same personality traits from prior lives and use them in your current life and in the afterlife?" "Only if they suit you," Shem replied. "You keep the ones that you like and discard the ones you don't."

My next two questions addressed whether the spirits had any mandate or gained any benefit from helping humans become more spiritual. I asked, "Do spirits on the other side use places like Brenda's church as a means to help people become spiritual?" "No, you make that happen," Shem said. "This is for your own good, not ours." "But does it help your aims and goals as a guide?" I asked. "Are you not responsible to a higher authority for our success?" Shem replied, "No, it's not like that. This is for your growth."

I was also curious about whether there truly was a heavenly "hall of records" where a person could review every moment of his prior lives. It was an important question to me; it might tell me where the details of my life as Otto came from. When I asked Shem about it, he said, "Yes, you can go there."

I then changed the focus and asked Shem a personal question. "What do you miss about being a human being on earth?" "My pipe," he replied.

Brenda once said that I had spent time as a Mayan priest, so I took the opportunity to ask Shem if I had lived any Native American lives. He said, "You tell me. What is in your heart?"

One of Dr. Newton's books talks about the possibility of merging your soul with God when in heaven to experience peace and great bliss. The souls in Dr. Newton's books seemed to suggest that this perk was available only to advanced souls. I decided to ask Shem about it.

"It is said that when you go back to heaven, you can merge yourself with God and experience tranquility. Can any soul do this, or do you have to be a higher soul?" "Any soul can go back to the Source," Shem answered.

At that point, my questions were exhausted, and I sincerely thanked him for sharing his answers. He then moved on to identify a woman in our group who was a 9/11 survivor. He described the terrible scene as an island surrounded by water with tall buildings. She was burdened with survivor's guilt, and Shem advised her to move on.

Somewhere in his time with us, Shem made the surprising assertion that we don't come to our current lives to learn lessons but rather to remember the lessons of prior lives. In reflecting upon his statement,

I realized that he could have been explaining why I was exploring the reincarnation highway at this point in my life.

At the end of the session, Shem struggled to physically stand up, explaining that he was not used to such a small body. (Greg's body is about the size of mine). He then motioned for everyone to stand up and went among us singing a Native American chant. He arranged everybody in a cross-like formation, the end of the points in the cross facing north, east, south, and west. He sat back down in his chair as everybody else kept standing in the cross formation with bewildered looks on their faces. Shem closed his eyes, and ten seconds later, Greg was back in his body. He opened his eyes and gazed at us in utter bewilderment, trying to figure out why everyone was standing in a cross formation and looking at him. The look on his face was priceless. I would also describe the experience that I had just gone through as priceless. I will meet Shem again in this story, but the next time I encounter him, he's going to give me a severe tongue-lashing.

# Chapter 10: The Story of Laurie

*The first and greatest punishment of the sinner is the conscience of sin.*
—Lucius Annaeus Seneca

## Reincarnation highway mile marker: Russian Front, 1941

In July of 1941 on the Russian Leningrad front, nineteen-year-old corporal Otto Kostermann of the Twenty-Third Grenadier Regiment of the German Wehrmacht was just outside a nondescript Russian village. He was busy digging a foxhole in a field near a rutted dirt road. Otto was a member of a company of men reduced during the summer's hard fighting related to Germany's recent invasion of Soviet Russia. Otto's squad of soldiers heard a column of vehicles approaching from the rear and turned to look. As the dusty column grew nearer, the soldiers saw that they were German vehicles but not from their own division. They were fast-moving motorcycles, scout cars, and a few armored half-tracks. The soldiers riding in the vehicles wore on their collars the double lightning-bolt runes of the infamous SS, the Nazi Party's army. Otto's best friend, Hans, remarked derisively, "Here comes the SS to save the day" as he recognized the Third Totenkopf insignia on the passing vehicles. Otto looked up at one of the passengers in the front seat of a passing half-track. The SS soldier had high cheekbones; piercing blue eyes; and blond, almost white, hair. Otto noted mentally that the SS soldier had such extraordinarily good looks that he would almost make a beautiful woman if his hair were long. The SS soldier turned his head and made eye contact with Otto as the SS half-track rushed by, and Otto returned to digging his foxhole, not giving this minor incident any further thought—that is, until he was reminded of this encounter sixty-eight years later.

Two German soldiers made eye contact in the middle of nowhere in 1941—what eventually happened to them? Chief Shem said that people spend most of their lives trying to remember the lessons of their prior life. What happens if one of them sinned badly in that prior life? Does the guilt go forward? If it does, how does it manifest? In this chapter, we will glimpse the answers to those questions.

With the move of the Mystic Nirvana to a storefront, an influx of new psychic students replaced most of the old group. Many of the new ones were younger and, frankly, did not need training as they were very talented. I think that the new ones joined not for the training but for the camaraderie, to meet weekly with people who had similar gifts and would feel comfortable talking openly about their unusual experiences.

One of Brenda's new students was a striking fortyish blonde named Laurie. When I first saw her, I thought that she looked very similar to Debby Harry of the rock group Blondie. Laurie had the same high cheekbones, blue eyes, and nearly white hair as the rock star. However, Laurie was a different kind of woman. She was an artist and had the quirky bohemian ways that many artists display as nonconformists who are not concerned about material things. She also seemed tormented to me, an intuition that came from observing her in class. She had a hard time keeping herself under control; she would often fidget and blurt out things. Brenda also had to work hard to keep her under control. Laurie seemed like a steam kettle boiling over, its internal pressure making the kettle shake and whistle, trying to find a way out.

Business people and artists have little in common; the two personalities almost repel each other like magnets with the same charge. As such, I really did not interact with Laurie in the beginning because we had nothing in common. However, one night she wore a Bundeswehr T-shirt ("the Bundeswehr" is Germany's name for its current army). The German T-shirt was just too provocative to me; I just had to say something to her. I spoke to her in German, thinking that she may speak the language. She recoiled in horror and told me that she just did not want to go there. I apologized, and she then explained that she had just gotten divorced from a German man and that she was going through a bad time as a result. With that, at least I broke the ice with her.

Further encounters with Laurie through the group showed her to be an extremely gifted and insightful psychic. She had all the psychic tools; she could see psychic visions as well as physically feel and hear messages from the other side. She would normally bring her elderly father, Jack, to our meetings. Jack is a very nice guy and very active for his age. He also has some psychic ability but nothing compared to his daughter's. As I befriended Jack, Laurie also warmed up to me and started passing along messages about my past lives from the other side, which I found very interesting and for which I was most appreciative. One of the most key things that she told me in an offhanded manner was that the black cross symbol had been a source of comfort to me in more than one past life. That would turn out to be very true for four of my past lives. With this comment, Laurie demonstrated that she had easy access to my past lives and was more tuned into my past than even Brenda was.

One night, after a training class at the Mystic Nirvana, I was talking to Laurie alone. She told me of the German WWII pistol collection that she had once had. *Oh, my God*, I thought. *She has the same affliction/ obsession that I have!* Luckily for her, it was not as bad as mine from the standpoint of sheer numbers. But still, it is just really unusual that a beautiful woman would have a German pistol collection. She told me that to rid herself of this obsession, she disposed of most of her pistols. In response, I brought a picture of my gun collection to show her the following week. Surprisingly, she was able to identify most of them by model. She was especially interested in the MP-40 machine guns on my wall. She warned me that most of my guns had blood on them (meaning that they had actually killed people) and that I should get rid of them. Knowing that we had a connection, I guess she felt comfortable with revealing the true reason she had an aversion to anything German. She told me her extraordinary story of being an SS soldier in World War II.

"Before the war," she began, "I was a gay man studying chemistry in a German university. I looked a lot like I do now, only I was a man. My name was Eric. I joined the SS in the late 1930s, and after my training, I served in the concentration camps. Ironically, a lot of us were gay in the SS. We were pulled out of guard duty at the concentration camps for the invasion of Russia. I had a lover in my unit, and we were together during the invasion. I belonged to a scouting unit where we would be way out in front of the main body of troops looking for the enemy. The gun that I used was the MP-40 submachine gun, like the ones in your collection. I have a vivid memory of my unit pulling into a Russian village. We were dusty, thirsty, and hungry. The villagers were happy to see us, and they gave us food and flowers. Much to my horror, my commanding officer then ordered us to shoot and kill all of the villagers because he thought they were partisans. I voiced my objections, but we massacred all the villagers as ordered. Later that night, I was still upset about it and complained to my lover about the atrocity we had just committed. I thought we were out of earshot. But someone else in our unit overheard our conversation and reported it to our commander. The next morning, I was summoned to report to him. He ordered me to kneel on the ground while he took his pistol out of his holster. He shot me from behind while I was on the ground. I remember being hit in the jaw and dying very quickly after being shot. I have this bitterness because I was betrayed by my fellow soldiers."

"Oh, my God. That is some story," I managed to reply.

"I had to tell you," said Laurie, "because I saw you back then in the war."

"Really?" I asked. "What unit were you in? Where did you fight?"

"I don't remember. This is something I don't want to remember. But I know I saw you. I was passing by you in a vehicle. Our eyes made contact; your eyes look exactly the same now as they were then except they were blue. I remember your eyes."

"Do you have any idea or clue what your unit was?"

"No," she replied, "but something sticks in my mind about the 'Kuban.'"

"The Kuban is in southern Russia," I said. "We couldn't have crossed paths as I was way up north in Leningrad."

"I know we crossed paths," Laurie said.

"Well, I don't know about that, but you should not be ashamed of your past. You actually did a brave thing by protesting to your commander. We both know what the penalty would be for doing something like that in the German Army, especially the SS. But you had the guts and the morals to do it. That speaks well of you."

"But I can't get over being betrayed by my comrades. That's what haunts me," she said.

"But still, you showed real courage. I admire that. I want you to know that I have no shame in my service in my division. We were an elite unit, and I am proud to have been a member. When I read about the tremendous obstacles and suffering that we endured, the whole idea that I lived through that just amazes me." Then, inspiration hit me.

"Laurie, I want to schedule a real reading from you," I said. "You really seem to be tapped into my background, much more than Brenda. It might help the both of us." Laurie was apprehensive because she was afraid of unlocking more of her past, but she agreed to give me a reading at the Mystic Nirvana the following Saturday.

In the meantime, I did a little research to see what SS units my army division would have encountered on the Leningrad front. Using a little bit of deduction, I knew that Russian villagers would not have offered gifts to invading German units beyond 1941 because of the suffering that the villagers endured at the hands of the Germans. That would mean that Laurie would have died early in the eastern front time period, probably 1941. Further research showed that only one SS division participated in the initial Northern Front invasion, the Totenkopf Division. *Totenkopf* translates to "death head" in German; not surprisingly, their division insignia was the skull and crossbones. Coincidentally, the Totenkopf Division was the *only* SS division that recruited its members from concentration camp guards. Another coincidence was that the Totenkopf Division was held in reserve during the initial invasion, staying behind the group that I was in. My group was initially in front of them on the march to the Stalin line. On the map, I could see that my division did pass through the Stalin line, but we were not the first unit through. The Totenkopf Division is credited with breaking through that Russian defensive position. This timing meant that it was very possible that the Totenkopf Division had passed through our positions on the way to the Stalin line, just like a car would pass another in the other lane on a highway. Another observation was that the Totenkopf Division was a motorized division that rode to battle, as opposed to my division, which had to walk or ride horse carts. All of these coincidences seem to offer some support to Laurie's claims that we had encountered each other in Russia—that is, if she was a member of the Totenkopf Division.

My appointment with Laurie was on a late Saturday morning. I walked into the Mystic Nirvana and found Laurie sitting in the front painting a fantastical picture. Bryan, a new member of the group, was sitting beside her and talking to her. I said hello to the both of them. Up to that point, I did not know how much psychic talent Bryan had, but I was about to find out. Bryan said, "I see that you have been busy."

"What do you mean?" I asked him.

"I see pictures of you working at your workbench, cutting things."

"That's true. I have been working on my gun collection," I said.

Just then Laurie turned from her painting and said, "They (meaning the spirits) tell me that you got your guns from the Sportsman's Guide."

*Hoo-boy*, I thought. *I just got a validation statement right out of the box.* I had not told anyone there that I reconditioned German guns, and I had never told anybody in this group about the Sportsman's Guide catalog and website. The first two guns of my collection had come from Sportsman's Guide! The Sportsman's Guide would be considered a hunter's catalog. Even though Laurie collected old German guns, she would never subscribe to or look for a hunting catalog because she was an animal lover. I could tell that the spirit world was already plugged into my upcoming reading and that the spirits were telling me that what Laurie was going to tell me was true.

I smiled and said, "I see that the spirits are showing off today. That's very good; I do get some of my guns from the Sportsman's Guide."

With that, Laurie put away her paints and led me back to one of the reading rooms. The room was dark with only a lit candle sitting in the middle of a table. I started off by telling her that I had done some research on which SS units I would have encountered in my past life as a German soldier and that the only one would have been the Totenkopf Division. "Were you a member of Totenkopf?" I asked. In response, Laurie burst into tears. "I did not want to remember this stuff," she said, "but yes, I was a member of Totenkopf. I see the death head symbol in my mind. I told you, I really did see you back then."

I didn't know what to say. I was sorry that she was upset and in pain. "Laurie, I want to learn more about my past, what I did back then, and how I felt. The spirit world is leading me down this path, and I want to find out why. Can you help me?"

Laurie composed herself and agreed to go on. To help her in the process of finding my WWII past, I had brought three German military medals that I had had a compulsion to buy a few months earlier from GunBroker.com. They were the Iron Cross for bravery, the Black Wound badge for suffering battle wounds, and the Winter Medal of 1941 for surviving the first winter in Russia. Since I had felt compelled to buy these medals, I assumed that the spirit world wanted me to have them because I was once awarded them. The trick was finding out how I had earned them. Laurie was so tapped into the spirit world that I knew I had an excellent chance of finding out.

I showed Laurie the German medals; she identified the Iron Cross and the Wound Badge but did not recognize the Winter Medal, perhaps because it was Laurie who was killed before that winter and who missed all the fun my comrades and I had. (Side note: The Winter Medal is the one the Germans called the frozen meat medal, as mentioned earlier, because most of the soldiers had to suffer through a brutal Russian winter with only their summer uniforms. Hitler mistakenly thought the Russians would be defeated before the winter, and thus the Army was not prepared for the cold.) Laurie started to pick up images of the prior owner of the Iron Cross and told me that this medal had been stripped off of his dead body on the western front by Americans. I told her that I am sure that the original owner would be happy that a former comrade like me would now own it as a replacement for the one that I had lost. She moved on to telling me how I earned these very medals. I will recount what she said in the next chapter, where I tell the story of Feldwebel (Sergeant) Otto. To relay the wartime story of Otto, I had to use Laurie's and my own psychic readings as sources as well as documented historical accounts.

Laurie did reveal some amazing things in addition to Otto's adventures. The most amazing thing was when she said that my girlfriend from my last life had been involved with me again in this life! She said that we had had a tumultuous relationship. (Yup, that's the exact word she used—*tumultuous*.) The first girl who popped into my mind was my first wife Julie; that relationship was definitely tumultuous.

"Was it my first wife, Julie?" I asked.

"No, you did not marry her," Laurie replied. "It was a girlfriend."

My mind raced to the second female on the short list of tumultuous relationships. "Was it my first girlfriend, Michele?"

"Yes, it was she."

My mind reeled at the possibility. "What was she like back then?"

"She was blonde with curly hair. She had a movie star look of that time. She was spirited. Most surprisingly of all, she was there to greet you in the white light in the moments after you died."

"You mean she died first? Was she killed in the fighting?"

"No, after you went off to war, she moved away from your hometown. She was shot by a man, a civilian. I think he was insane."

"Was she involved with him?"

"No."

*Amazing*, I thought. I found all of this just amazing. (Much later, I found out the real reason that Lana and her family moved away. They did not go voluntarily. Throughout the war, the Nazis performed ethnic cleansing operations against the Polish population. In 1942, East Prussian Gauleiter (Nazi governor) Erich Koch helped implement Generalplan Ost, under which more than one million Poles were expelled from German territory. More than likely, Lana's family ended up in the Ukraine, which was still under German control. I could only imagine Otto's reaction to the fact that the Nazis expelled his girlfriend while he was away at war.) We will come back to Michele later.

An extremely important piece of information that Laurie gave me was her confirmation of Brenda's reading that I had been a German bishop once and that, as bishop, I had been stabbed. Here was another nudge by the spirit world to pursue my past as a cleric.

The last thing she picked up was Karol's miscarriage fifteen years before. She said she knew it because she felt the (psychic) pain in her abdomen that mimicked Karol's. Now I was starting to feel bad again for Laurie because she was really being put through the wringer for me. At the end of the reading, I gave her a big hug and thanked her profusely.

A few weeks later, Laurie did me the service of performing another reading that was short but very meaningful. As a demonstration, Brenda hypnotized Laurie while everybody was sitting in a circle of folding chairs. Brenda then directed Laurie to walk around to each person in the circle and give him or her a message from the spirits. The message that Laurie gave me was that I was going to receive the ability to speak to the spirits whenever I wanted. A few minutes later, we performed an exercise in which we wrote a question on a folded sheet of paper. Naturally, the question that I wrote on my piece of paper was, "When will I get this gift of being able to speak to the spirits?" There were at least fifteen people in the class that day. We each wrote our own question, folded the paper slip, and put the folded paper in a bowl. Each person then reached into the bowl and picked out one slip without looking at it. The purpose of the exercise was for each person to answer the written question without looking at the note. Of course, Laurie had picked mine without knowing it was mine. (Isn't it amazing how these things are arranged?) Laurie gave this answer to my question: "There is no need to struggle for your struggle is causing you to sink deeper. Relax and let life flow, for it is in life's flow that your answers will come. Be quiet now and wait. Go inside and be patient for that is your answer."

Laurie was insightful enough to write down this message after she said it so that I would have a record of it. The answer was perfect for me. After my rocket-fast entry into the psychic world, my abilities had leveled out. I have been impatient for months to obtain the ability to hear and see psychically. My expected clairvoyant and clairaudient abilities were not showing up yet despite Brenda's assurances that all it took was meditation and training. But shortly thereafter, I could ask a question to the universal consciousness *without* being in a meditative state and receive a head-shake answer. Laurie called it right again.

# Chapter 11: Finding Sergeant Otto

*Of course, the outcome of the war would not have been changed. The war was lost, perhaps, when it was started. At least it was lost in the winter of '42, in Russia.*

—Adolf Galland

## Reincarnation highway mile marker: Russian front, World War II

In this chapter, I reveal what happened in my immediate past life. Did World War II memories come rushing back to me in this process? No, that was not the case. I received only facts devoid of feelings, not real memories. It took some work to recover this information, and it came in waves over a period of a few months. I used Laurie's psychic readings as a framework and then laid them over written historical accounts of what my army division did in World War II. The book *Weg und Schicksal der 11.Infantrie Division* (*The Way and Fate of the 11th Infantry Division*) written by Werner Buxa in 1961 was my main historical source. Unfortunately for me, the book was available only in German, so I had to painstakingly translate the sections I needed for research. (Let's just say that this exercise greatly improved my German). I also went into meditation many times to verify where and when the events that Laurie described took place. I have put together the following background information as an overview so that Laurie's readings could be put into historical context.

Otto Kostermann was born on May 5, 1922, in the town of Mandeln, a farm suburb of the Prussian capital city of Konigsberg. Otto's hometown was located in the far eastern German province of East Prussia, on the border of Lithuania. Prussia was the long-time home of Germany's finest soldiers and many of its political leaders. However, this area also had a diverse population in that a large community of Polish people also lived there. The Poles tended to be the workers, while the German Prussians made up the higher caste of Prussian society.

Otto was the third son of Dieter and Laura Kostermann, and the family owned a large farm and was fairly prosperous. Otto had plans to become a farmer because he was being groomed to take over the farm from his father. In his late teens, Otto had a sweetheart named Lana, who came from a Polish family. She was a very pretty blonde, and Otto was very taken with her. Otto dreamed of taking over the farm and marrying Lana, but that was not to be. In 1939, Germany invaded Poland, and World War II started. As a healthy young man, Germany would require that he serve in the armed forces for the duration of the war.

Germany's large army (the Wehrmacht) was divided into over two hundred 12,000-man units called divisions, and each division was geographically based and drafted its men locally. Otto's oldest brother, Oscar, was drafted into the local Eleventh Infantry Division in time for the invasion of Poland. Unfortunately, Oscar died in that invasion. The next Kostermann brother was drafted into the air force. Otto's turn came in 1940 at the age of eighteen, when he was also drafted into the Eleventh Division. As Otto's hometown of Mandeln was closest to the town of Rastenburg, he was assigned to the Twenty-Third Regiment of the Eleventh Division. There he trained to be a rifleman with the other draftees of his class of eighteen-year-olds. The rifle that Otto was given was the Mauser 98-K, the same rifle model that I was compelled to buy for my collection. In his class, there was a young man named Hans M. who became one of his closest mates. After completing his intense training, Otto went home on a short leave to spend time with his family and Lana. After this leave, Otto joined the ranks of the Twenty-Third Regiment as a private in the winter of 1941. He would go home to Mandeln only one more time, when he returned in 1943 on medical leave and attended sergeant's school in nearby Allenstein.

Otto's wartime adventures started on June 6, 1941, when his entire division left its barracks and moved to its concealed attack positions on the border with Russia. At 3:05 a.m. on June 22, the massive German invasion of Russia began. After a German artillery barrage on the Russian border positions, Otto and his comrades started to walk across the border.[1] The men of the Eleventh Division were a subunit of the one-million-man-strong Army Group North, whose mission was to march several hundred miles across hostile territory and capture Russia's second-largest city, Leningrad (now St. Petersburg). This German army group reached the city in a matter of months and surrounded it for nine hundred days, but they never captured it. During this time in Russia, the German soldiers experienced extreme cold while living outside, horribly unsanitary conditions, and constant warfare against a much larger Russian army. What was the payoff for enduring these miserable conditions for four years? Absolutely zero. Sadly, *none* of the men of the Eleventh Division or their families would ever live in East Prussia again, even after the war ended four years later. They would be either dead or evicted by the Russians.

As for Otto's personal experiences in the war, I will give selected passages from Laurie's psychic readings and then add context to them from my other sources. You will notice something unusual about Laurie's use of pronouns in her readings—specifically, she treated the personalities of Otto and me (Frank) as one interchangeable person by repeatedly using the word *you*. Don't be confused by this word usage, but use it as, perhaps, a confirmation that Otto and Frank are the same person. One other note—to provide support that this narrative is plausible, footnotes tie the psychic readings to the written historical accounts.

*Laurie talks about us meeting in the past life:* I (Laurie) was an SS soldier in WWII. We briefly came into contact with each other during the war.[2]

*Laurie talks about my growth as a soldier and the losses that were experienced:* You (Otto) were a farmer and not a warrior to start. But you became a warrior. You survived because you were very intuitive on the battlefield, almost psychic. You had great survival skills because on that battlefield it was truly survival of the fittest. Several times, your unit lost half its men in the fighting, but you survived. Once you were crossing a bridge and were ambushed. Russian machine guns and mortars wiped out half of your squad. Later, there was another battle where again your unit lost half its men.[3]

*Context:* Otto belonged to an elite unit that was often used as a "fire brigade" to try to stop Russian breakthrough attacks. These elite German units usually held the enemy back but suffered high rates of death and wounded.

The German Northern Army Group effectively surrounded Leningrad and cut off its food supplies in the fall of 1941. Almost two million Russian civilians were trapped. The Russian Army desperately attacked the Germans to the south of Leningrad in several large-scale attempts to break through and rescue the citizens of the city. In 1942, Otto participated in two large battles in which the number of causalities was horrific. Otto's unit did lose half of its men in the second 1942 battle, but the Russians suffered worse and did not break through. Yet, despite all of the carnage around him, Otto got through both battles without a scratch. (I guess he knew where not to be at a particular moment.) With all the losses in his unit, Otto was promoted to take the place of those squad leaders who had been killed or wounded. Now, he would be responsible for leading a small group of young replacement soldiers as a noncommissioned officer.[4]

*Laurie tells of how Otto was decorated for bravery:* This is how you won your Iron Cross. Partisan units were attacking your supply lines, making life miserable for your division. Yours and other squads were sent to fan out across the countryside to hunt down the partisans. During a hunting patrol, you and your squad did encounter a group of six or seven partisans who were on top of a hill. While your men fired on them to keep their attention, you exchanged your submachine gun for the squad's large MG42 machine gun. You worked your way to another hill behind the partisans, where they could not see you, and started to fire on them. The MG42 was new to the battlefield at that time. It shot so fast that it made a strange ripping noise that the civilian partisans had never heard before. They were so surprised by it that they actually stood up to see what it was. That made it easier for you to shoot them down. Since you had the partisans pinned down, the rest of your squad worked their way up the hill, and they finished them off by throwing hand grenades into their position. For your actions, you were awarded the Iron Cross, 2nd Class.[5]

*Otto flanking the partisan position with a borrowed machine gun.*

I find it amazing how well Laurie's reading dovetails with the account that I gave in the hypnoregression session with Brenda, described in Chapter 8. What's even more amazing is that my gun wall at home memorialized this story before I knew it. An MG42 machine gun hangs in the center of the wall with a German "potato masher" hand grenade resting on top of it. Pinned on the wall above the MG42 is an Iron Cross, Second Class medal. Like Chopra wrote, there are no coincidences.

Linking this paragraph with the next one, what better way could there be to "blood," or give experience to, the new soldiers under my charge than to put them into action against nonregular soldiers like the partisans? These young soldiers were going to need all of the experience they could get before going through the meat grinder of a battle that was coming next.

I asked Laurie how I was awarded the Black Wound badge, and she responded, "I see you in a bunker with four other soldiers. A shell explodes, and two men are instantly killed. You are wounded on the right side in the face, arm, torso, and leg." I also asked her how my good friend Hans had died. She said, "He was shot and killed during street fighting."

The process of recovering my past life had provided me only with facts, no memories and certainly no feelings. Laurie reported that my best friend had been shot and killed; just saying that without any accompanying feeling just seems cold and abstract. How did I feel about it? How did I react? For the purposes of this book, it seems that it is only right to try to re-create Otto's feelings about the loss to honor Hans. (In Chapter 15, actual emotions from the war do seep into my current life.) The only way to replicate this feeling would be to borrow a quote from another German soldier who wrote about the loss of his best friend on the Russian Front. This excerpt is from the book *Frontsoldaten*. I am pretty confident that Otto felt the same.

> Now that the last and dearest of my old comrades are gone, I can no longer get rid of the feeling of loneliness. I am now one of the few still present from the summer of 1941. The bodies of the fallen lay there, rigid and lifeless, wrapped in canvas. I sadly thought, "He cared for me as a comrade and brother and friend in past times. He fought alongside me, starved and froze with me and shared the concerns and distress of the soldier experience. He marched next to us and now he has fallen. "Not only will your spirit and your memory live on, you yourself now live in another, better world." We said our final goodbye and then marched on to the front. I felt I left a piece of me behind.

My only consolation was that I still had my squad, and that means infinitely much.

Both of the last two events described by Laurie happened during the Russian Operation Spark offensive of January 1943. The Russians amassed an overwhelming force of men just south of Leningrad. They desperately wanted to push the Germans back so that they could reopen a railroad line that connected the city to the rest of Russia. The initial attack opened with great success for the Russians; they trapped a large group of German troops behind their lines. Someone had to rescue the German units that were in trouble. The Eleventh Division was ordered to march thirty miles in winter weather to help throw back the Russian attack. Its soldiers knew something was up because they could hear the rumble of cannon fire far to the north. My reference book noted that just before the division moved out, the officers looked somewhat anxiously at the young soldiers who had just arrived to replace last year's losses. They feared that, because the replacements had received hardly any baptism of fire, they might not be ready for what awaited them. As only 40 percent of the division's units had trucks to transport the troops for this journey, Otto and his Twenty-Third Regiment had to walk the whole way to the town of Mga. Another problem was that the supply column carrying their ammunition was traveling far behind them, so they went into battle with only the ammunition and food that they carried. As the men approached the battle area of Mga Station, they were already exhausted from the lack of food and sleep. Passing through the town, they were fired upon by Russian snipers and took some casualties, one of which was Otto's friend Hans. The troops continued to move on to their objective of Hill 43.3, where the Russians had established themselves at the top. Otto belonged to the one-hundred-man Fifth Company of the second battalion; the sister Sixth Company was marching down the same road in front of Otto's company. The Sixth Company had the honor of attacking the hill first during the night in a heavy snowstorm. The Russian fire was so heavy from the top of the hill that the Sixth Company was almost wiped out, with only a few survivors making it back to the bottom. Otto's Fifth Company and its other sister company, the Seventh, attacked the same Russian hilltop position at daybreak. Still low on ammunition, Otto and his squad charged up the hill. The heavy Russian gunfire and mortar fire forced Otto and five of his men to take cover behind a small knoll on the hill for protection. Otto was just starting to look to his right when a large Russian mortar shell exploded among his group. The two soldiers to his right were killed instantly, and Otto was wounded in several places and knocked unconscious. He woke up later in a hospital tent. Because of their lack of ammunition, the rest of Otto's comrades fell back from the hill under heavy fire. On the morning of February 2, the rest of the Eleventh Division was ordered to move into the Hill 43.3 area. The Eleventh Division did plug the gap in the lines, but the Russians were successful in pushing the Germans back far enough that the railroad line could be reopened. The people of Leningrad were finally saved. The Eleventh Division again lost over half of its men in this single battle. The division was so devastated that it was pulled out of the line and sent to Greece so that it could rest and recover with new replacement troops. Otto spent six weeks in the hospital and was sent home to Mandeln to heal. After his recovery, instead of joining his unit in Greece, he was sent to sergeants school during the summer of 1943. He would rejoin his unit in the Leningrad area just in time for the next bloodbath.

*Laurie talks about difficult times when Otto and his small group were surrounded and cut off:* You and your men were marching to a city. You were cut off from communication with your superiors and were down to only six men and two horses. There was bitter cold, and some of the men were suffering from foot rot. Everyone was hungry. You had to kill one of the horses for food. The Russians were in pursuit and trying to catch you and your men. One time your group had to hide in a ravine or hole in the side of a snowy hill until the Russians passed by without seeing you. You survived and saved your men through savvy and guile. It was truly a case of survival of the fittest. You gave courage to your men so that they could endure. You were loved and looked up to by your comrades.

The above reading doesn't even begin to communicate the emotions involved in experiencing this horrifying situation. The emotions felt by Otto's men would be sheer terror combined with a big dose of misery. The Soviet Union had three times the population and industrial capacity of Germany. As the war went into its third year, the German forces got weaker, and the Russians become overwhelmingly stronger. Eventually, the Germans could no longer hold the Russians forces back. The Russians launched a massive attack in January 1944 on the Leningrad front, and the whole front utterly broke open. Whole German divisions of men were vaporized or thrown headlong into retreat. The roads were jammed with retreating German troops; equipment, wagons, and vehicles were abandoned everywhere. Otto's division was ordered to hold off the hordes of attacking Russians in the sector assigned to them while the rest of the army hightailed it to somewhere safer. It seemed like a suicide mission, but the high command's expectations were for the Eleventh Division to hold off the Russians while retreating in an organized manner to the city of Pleskau.

How did things turn out for Otto? Once again, the Eleventh was successful, but it lost many men in this retreat. Normally, lieutenants commanded platoons of forty men, but the losses of officers in the prior years had been so high that Otto was assigned a platoon of twenty-six men to command at the start of the battle. The plan was to spread the division in a long defensive line, fight, and then keep leapfrogging backward in coordination with the other units of the division. All units were to keep in contact with and support one another. In the beginning, this maneuver worked, but as the days wore on, the losses became staggering. The artillery fire and bombing from the Russian air force took a tremendous toll.

On January 24, the Twenty-Third Regiment's commander, Colonel Kolberg, was killed in action. When a colonel gets killed in close combat, you know that things are going very badly for your side. The fast-moving Russians kept getting behind the spread-out German units to the point that even the commanding general of Otto's division was lightly wounded in the thick of a firefight. As time went on, shrinking units lost contact with one another, and they were on their own. Supplies were cut off, and the surviving units had only the food and ammunition that they were carrying on their supply horses. As Laurie said, Otto's platoon was down to only six men and two horses. They were hungry, frozen, and running for their lives. The modern reader might think, *Why not give up and surrender?* That was not a viable option. First, the Russians were likely to shoot and kill anyone who surrendered. Even if they did accept a surrender, the captured German soldiers would be shipped immediately to slave labor camps in Siberia where they would be fed a starvation diet and worked to death in the cold. As an example, of the ninety thousand German soldiers who were captured at Stalingrad in 1943, only five thousand made it home to Germany years later. Surrender meant death; Otto's squad had no choice but to go on. Under this extreme duress, strong emotional ties of comradeship were strengthened to an almost mystical level. Let me again borrow from the book *Frontsoldaten* to describe this feeling in a similar circumstance: "The constant feeling of being threatened, the sense of being stalked, and the fear of being killed or captured at any moment produced intense feelings of terror and the overwhelming desire to be part of the security of comradeship."

Bridging the gap to Laurie's upcoming last revelation, Otto and his remaining six men made it back to the German lines and rejoined the division in mid–February 1944. From there, they were trucked to the city of Pleskau and given a well-deserved short rest and warm food.

*Otto and the remains of his platoon in retreat; down*
*to six men and a horse, February 1944*

You would think that perhaps the fighting spirit of the Twenty-Third Regiment would be smothered after that costly retreat, but that was not the case. In March, the Russians attacked again, crossing the Narva River in Estonia and occupying an area across the river. Wikipedia has an article describing this battle, and Otto's Twenty-Third Regiment is specifically mentioned in it, saying they counterattacked the Russians, working side by side with an SS tank force and throwing the Russians back across the river. Another online article about this battle describes the Twenty-Third Regiment as being "superb." The *Way and Fate* book describes the regiment's capturing an immense amount of food supplies from the Russians in this battle, supplies that were greatly appreciated by the troops. Of special interest to the troops was the large quantity of canned American bacon that the Russians had, which the German troops later enjoyed. They marveled that the Americans were rich enough to send their allies good food halfway across the world, while the German soldiers ate poorly. (I wonder if this admiration of American richness had an impact on Otto's soul when it was considering where to live in its next life?) The Wikipedia article ends with this comment about the condition of the Russian and German forces on the Narva front in Estonia at the end of April 1944: "The losses exhausted the strengths of both sides. For May and June, the front stagnated with the exception of the artillery, air, sniper activity and clashes between reconnaissance platoons." A clash between reconnaissance troops is what would lead to Otto's death at the Narva battlefield.

Finally, I asked Laurie to describe how I died. She responded, "You led a small patrol of two other men on a night patrol.[6] Your mission was to locate the current positions of the Russians. You were approaching a two-story farmhouse when shots rang out. You were hit in the leg. The three of you ran to the farmhouse for cover. The farmhouse had a set of outside stairs that led to a door. You limped up the steps and were the second man through that door. You did not know it, but there were Russians inside. As you came through the door, a Russian sprang at you with a bayonet, yelling, "Die, *swinehund!*" The bayonet plunged into the front of your left shoulder and chest. You sunk to the floor and died quickly. As your soul left your body, you looked down on your body and thought, *I didn't see that coming.* As you went into the white light, Lana was one of the souls there to welcome you.

I found it amazing that Laurie's account of Otto's death matched the hypnoregression account of my death in Chapter 8. It also matched Tony's description of the residual energy left by the bayonet in my left shoulder when he was working on my shoulder injury. Where did the spirit of Sergeant Otto go after he left his body in that Estonian farmhouse? I think the best explanation comes from a quote in the book *Eastern Front Combat.* The memory is that of Joachim Stempel, who was a young German lieutenant trapped at Stalingrad in 1943. Ironically, his father was a general who had also been trapped there. Stempel recounted his last conversation with his father just before he went into captivity. "Now it will end here, and I cannot express how much I despair." At this my father laid his hand on my shoulder and said, "It's all right, my boy! Shortly, we'll meet again up there, where all brave soldiers find their peace and quiet. Go with God!"

*Otto's death in an Estonian farmhouse*

I think the general had it exactly right. On that night of May 1, 1944, Otto closed his eyes for the last time and went to that higher vibration called heaven. He enjoyed twelve and one-half years in that higher vibrational level until he opened his eyes again in Berea, Ohio, on an October night in 1956. The only difference was that his name was no longer Otto; he was now named Frank—different name, different body, but his spirit was and is exactly the same.

FOOTNOTES:

(1)     While Germany was famous for its fast-moving blitzkrieg tanks, Otto's unit had no tanks and very few motorized vehicles. All of the supplies and baggage for the Eleventh Division were moved by a very large number of horse-drawn wagons. The soldiers had to walk, and officers rode on their individual horses. As such, this long column of men and horse wagons crossed the border.

(2)     Page 33 of the *Way and Fate of the 11th Division* does make reference to a false report that an SS unit joined the Eleventh Division on July 21 to fight together on the same battlefield. The only SS unit in the entire Leningrad battlefront at that time was Eric's/Laurie's. This is just conjecture on my part, but I think the reason for that false report was that that particular SS unit actually did pass through the Eleventh Division's area of operations on that date but did not stay.

(3)     The German army in WWII was renowned for the fighting quality of its soldiers, but even among this good group of soldiers, there was a higher level of soldier. Otto belonged to the higher level. The German army developed a system that rated the effectiveness of its individual divisions based on hardness, endurance, skill and steadiness of leadership, fighting spirit, training standards, and dependability. High ratings were given only to divisions that had repeatedly proved themselves in these areas over a sustained period. The divisions that always scored the elite rating were the First, Fifth, Seventh, Eighth, Eleventh, Twenty-First, and Twenty-Eighth Divisions. Otto and the Eleventh fought two huge battles in 1942, the Wolchow River pocket in January and the Kirischi bridgehead in June. Both battles were huge bloodbaths for both sides. Otto's unit did lose half of its men at Kirischi, but the Russians lost far more men and did not break through.

(4)     Squad leaders (like Otto) were assigned the MP-40 submachine gun as their standard weapon; regular soldiers were issued Mauser 98-K rifles. The MP-40 is

the favorite and most numerous weapon in my current gun collection. I have three nonworking ones and a fourth that I actually shoot. I guess you could say that I have a strong, lingering attachment to that gun. I am sure that it saved my prior life many times.

(5) Partisans were armed Russian citizens and soldiers trapped behind the German lines. They lived hidden in the forest and came out to attack vulnerable German truck and horse wagon supply convoys. The Russian government went through much effort to keep the partisans armed because they were very effective in tying down German troops. Partisans caused the German army major trouble, and it was very common to go on antipartisan patrols to try to eliminate that never-ending problem. Page 47 of the *Way and Fate of the 11th Division* shows a map of partisan activity during the Leningrad campaign. Sure enough, there is a large blotch of partisan activity on the map right behind the area where the Eleventh Division was in the fall of 1942.

(6) Nighttime patrols into enemy territory were standard operating procedure for both the Germans and the Russians. The Germans thought nothing of risking highly experienced junior officers and noncommissioned officers to get the valuable information obtained in these patrols.

# Chapter 12: Hey, I Used to Be Famous!

*Nearly all men can stand adversity, but if you want to test a man's character, give him power.*

—Abraham Lincoln

## Reincarnation highway mile marker: Cologne, Germany, thirteenth century

I had reached the first waypoint on the reincarnation highway. I had discovered what I had done in my immediate prior life as Otto. *Where do I go from here?* I wondered. *Do I stop or press on?* The "other side" had given me two nudges to explore my supposed life as a bishop. I appreciated the encouragement, but I would have followed that trail anyway— I knew that being a bishop in medieval times meant that I would have been a rich and powerful man. I also knew that there was a good possibility that there would be some written historical record of me, which would be exciting to discover. So I went in search of who I had been, using my meager psychic abilities. The next leg on the reincarnation highway was going to be more like *The Da Vinci Code,* where I would follow leads and clues to find my identity as a bishop.

The clues I had were sparse; Brenda's information led me to look in the medieval period. The second clue came from one of my first psychic meditations, which revealed that I had been German for the past thousand years. Laurie gave me the last two relevant clues—that I had been stabbed as a bishop and that the black cross was a symbol of comfort to me. With these clues, I started my search. Using the clue of death by stabbing, I assumed that this bishop must have been killed on the battlefield defending his city or while with a German king on a crusade to the Middle East, so I Googled "German military bishops." On the first page of results was a website that had a list of approximately thirty German military bishops. This cut down the number of bishop prospects to something much more manageable.

To winnow down the list of thirty bishops, I used my new gift of being able to contact the spirits at any time. This new capability allowed me to look at a list of names in a book or on a computer screen and have the spirits tell me which name was the one I was looking for. I looked at the list of thirty names on the screen and mentally called off each name. I received a lot of *no*s until I reached the fourteenth bishop on the list, when I was rewarded with a *yes*. It was Konrad von Hochstaden of Cologne, born 1205, died 1261. "Are you sure that I was this man?" I asked psychically. The answer was an affirmative head shake. I Googled this specific name and was rewarded with a lot of hits. Old Konrad, it seems, got into all kinds of mischief and trouble. One of the first websites I investigated had a picture of Konrad's statue (or should I say, my statue) on the wall of the famous Cologne Cathedral.

*Konrad's irreverent statue on the wall of the Cologne*
*Cathedral. Photography by Raymond User.*

However, the website was not a historical one but a buzz-kill comedy website with weird pictures and stories. Konrad's picture was labeled "Konrad von Moonz." The reason for that description was readily apparent. If you looked at the statue itself, he looked pretty impressive in his clerical garb. But since the statue was high on a wall, it had to stand on a small pedestal, and right below the pedestal supporting the statue was a smaller figurine of a bent-over monk pulling up his robe, mooning the public below. Not only was this monk smiling, he was performing an impossible sexual act on himself. Let's just say that it was something that only male dogs can do. I just burst out laughing in front of the computer. Again asking psychically if I was really this guy, I again received the confirming head shake. *Ho-boy*, I thought. If this is my legacy, I had to really tick off a lot of people for them to go through the effort of creating this nasty, profane statue. In comparison, the statue of the bishop to Konrad's left has three monkeys playing bongo drums, and the one to his right featured a figure of a monk carving a log. I got the strong impression that Konrad was something special but not in a good way. One individual posted a comment on the website that the statue was well deserved as Konrad was well known for screwing over his friends.

Another website revealed Konrad's coat of arms, as shown below:

As you can see, it was just as Laurie foretold in her reading, detailed in Chapter 12, when she said that I always took comfort in the symbol of the black iron cross. Well, this segment of the reincarnation highway kept getting more and more interesting. But had I really been Konrad?

Being an amateur historian, I really dove into my research on Konrad. I actually found an entire academic book written in German about Konrad, in addition to several historical articles that referred to him. As I found out that he was much more powerful than the average archbishop, I possessed a strong desire to have been this man. In this fresh view of the universe that I discovered, I knew that people live many, many lives. For almost all souls, most of those lives are humble and difficult. But once in a while, you get an opportunity to live at the very top and do fantastic, exciting things. Whether you are bad or good according to the Christian standard does not matter. What matters is the experience and the thrill of the ride. And Konrad's ride was a legitimate E ticket. In having an opportunity to have been Konrad, I knew that that particular life would have been one of the crown jewels in my collection of lives.

Before I tell you more about Konrad, I need to set the stage historically so that you can understand how different times were then. To do so, I want to give you some flexibility regarding how deeply you personally want to go into this topic. Just like in the Sergeant Otto chapter, I will footnote the deep, historical stuff. The historical record does tie in with the psychic messages that I received; you, however, might just choose to take my word for it if you do not like or want to delve into the historical material. If you want to, have at it and read the footnotes. Anyway, Konrad was much, much more than just rich. It turned out that he was also one of the most powerful politicians in the Holy Roman Empire because he was one of the seven electors who could elevate a king to the office of emperor. His status as an elector required people to address him as "Your Serene Highness." Not only was Konrad a powerful politician, he was also a warrior prince who was extremely aggressive with his own personal army. This type of behavior is certainly very different from that of modern Catholic Bishops. So why the difference? To explain, the historian Benjamin Arnold wrote,

The majority of bishops in medieval Germany were born into aristocratic or knightly families who prided themselves in their proficiency in warfare. In spite of the message of the Gospels and the training received for high clerical office, it was not surprising that bishops retained their nobleman's instinct as warriors when they became priests. The German bishops may have been remarkably talented in the peacetime execution of their office, but their military spirit remained an inseparable part of their religious administration.[1]

From this, I picture Konrad as both a knight and a priest, an interesting mixture of jobs. But what was he really like? Historians called Konrad *"vir furiosus et bellicosus"* (a man furious and warlike), and the annals of his time are full of praise for the aggressive tactics by which Konrad outfought his princely rivals in the archdiocese.[2] A modern translation of his personality would be angry and violent. Giving an angry, violent man his own army sounds like a volatile combination that could have ignited some fireworks. Did it? Examine his historical actions below and judge for yourself:

1. In a war between the pope and the German emperor, Konrad initially fought for the emperor but switched sides to the pope's. Konrad's changing sides resulted in his being wounded and captured in battle against the emperor's allies. He was thrown into a dungeon and held captive for eight months until he escaped.
2. Konrad's rule over the city of Cologne was a series of struggles with neighboring princes and with the citizens of Cologne, who refused to acknowledge his authority. Konrad was generally victorious, but his often treacherous manner of warfare has left many dark spots on his reputation.
3. Konrad knew how to pull political strings to get his patrons elected to the emperor position. When Pope Innocent IV deposed Emperor Frederick II (July 17, 1245), it was chiefly due to the influence of Konrad that the pope's candidate, Henry Raspe of Thuringia, was elected emperor. When Henry died after a short reign of seven months (February 17, 1247), it was again the influence of Konrad that placed the crown on the head of the youthful William of Holland.
4. Konrad was not above using his office as elector for personal gain. After the death of Emperor William (January 28, 1256), Konrad played an important role in the election of the

new emperor. For a large sum, he sold his vote to Richard of Cornwall, son of the infamous Prince John of *Robin Hood* fame, and crowned him at Aachen on May 17, 1257.

To "flesh out the many dark spots on his character," let me reprise a story from the recent novel *Death and the Devil* that uses Archbishop Konrad as one of its characters. You can really see what kind of treacherous person he was.

To gain more power in the city of Cologne, Konrad removed all mint officials from their offices, claiming that they had exceeded their powers. That meant the city could issue no more coins. The merchants screamed bloody murder about this abrupt change and the adverse impact it would have on their trade. The political rivals of the merchants were the city's unions, and they saw an opportunity to gain power over the merchants. The unions then made an official complaint to Konrad about the city judges, who mostly came from mercantile families. In response to the union complaint, Konrad dismissed all the judges except for one. He then decreed that in the future, he would make all appointments to the council of judges himself. With this move, the merchants lost all of their political power. Konrad then accused the merchant families of serious crimes and summoned them to a hearing. He then banished the twenty-five merchants who refused to attend the hearing. They had to flee the city; otherwise, the mob would have torn them to pieces.

Then Konrad appointed new judges, one or two merchants among them but mostly craftsman and guild masters. Several months later, the merchants brought charges against the new judges, demanding that they be removed from office. Konrad was diplomatic and promised a fair hearing. In the hearing, he tried to reach a compromise between the two parties, but the merchants did not want to compromise. In the meantime, the unions had gathered an armed mob outside the court house. The merchants responded immediately by also arming themselves and then marching on Konrad's palace because they suspected Konrad of inciting the unions against them. The merchants then barricaded Konrad in his palace by setting up roadblocks in front of the two separate entrances. Konrad called out his armed guard, and a pitched battle almost started. Here is where Konrad used his legendary trickery. He sent peace envoys to the front door of the rebel merchant's barricades, offering an unarmed meeting in the palace to discuss terms. He told the merchant rebels that the merchants at the back door of the palace had already accepted this offer. He used the very same trick with the barricading merchants at the back door. Both groups of merchants fell for the trick. As Konrad promised the merchants safe conduct, the merchants, in good faith, went inside unarmed and were immediately arrested by Konrad's armed guards. Twenty-four merchants were thrown into the dungeon while the others fled the city for their safety. Konrad invited the escapees to another meeting, but of course they were not so stupid as to fall for another trick, nor did Konrad want them to. It gave him the excuse to also banish them, which he did with the Pope's blessing.

Well, what can I say? This guy played to win. In modern times, no one would ever believe that someone like him could have existed. There is no modern example of Konrad. Then I realized that there was a modern fictional character that seemed pretty close. For those of you who know the *Star Wars* story, Konrad reminds me of the evil Count Dooku. He was the character who defeated Obi-Wan and Anakin in battle in *Episode Two* and was killed by Anakin in *Episode Three*. Just for fun, let's compare the two.

| Trait | Count Dooku | Konrad |
|---|---|---|
| 1. Has cool title | Yes—Count | Yes—"Your Serene Highness" |
| 2. Leads an army of thugs | Yes | Yes |
| 3. Regular people grovel before him | Yes | Yes |
| 4. Feared by his enemies | Yes | Yes |
| 5. All about power and nothing but power | Yes | Yes |
| 6. Very proficient with a light saber or sword | Yes | Yes |
| 7. Very connected to the emperor | Yes | Yes |
| 8. Heavily protected by security | Yes—robot droids | Yes—palace guards |
| 9. Married with children | No way | No way |

| Trait | Count Dooku | Konrad |
|---|---|---|
| 10. Invades or attacks other worlds or lands to expand his power | Yes | Yes |
| 11. Throws captured enemies into the dungeon | Yes | Yes |
| 12. Can invoke the supernatural power of the universe to advance his cause | Yes—the force | Yes—threatens damnation by God (and people believed he had the power to bring that about) |
| 13. Will use trickery to win | Yes | Yes—it's fun that way and costs less! |
| 14. The good guys plot against him | Yes | Yes |
| 15. Can hurl large boulders at enemies through the use of mind power | Yes | Sadly, no |
| 16. Died by the sword | Yes | ? |

Dooku died by the sword, but did Konrad? What is interesting about Wikipedia's biography of Konrad is that it simply states that Konrad died on September 28, 1261. It does not say how he died. According to the several psychic readings I received, as a bishop I supposedly died violently by stabbing. There is no mention of how Konrad died in the historical record. I consulted other web pages and received the exact same information about his death. In each source, there was a definitive date of death but had not a clue or whisper about how he died. The academic book written in German about Konrad's reign is offered online by the Toronto Library, and when I translated its page that documents his death, I found it to also be mysteriously silent about how he had died. Based upon Konrad's reputation, it would not surprise me at all to learn that some powerful person had him killed, since he did not die in battle. I would especially suspect the rich merchant families of Cologne. Cologne was Germany's largest city at the time, with about fifty thousand people. Konrad had a long struggle with the townspeople when he tried to deprive the city of its independence. In 2005, the German author Frank Schatzing wrote a historical novel called *Death and the Devil*, which was about how the surviving Cologne merchants plotted revenge against Konrad for banishing their family members and friends. The plotline of this book centered on a plan to kill Archbishop Konrad using a deadly assassin who had just gotten back from the Crusades. The novel ends with the assassination attempt being unsuccessful. The author mentions at the end of his book that when Konrad did finally die, the merchants escaped from his dungeon. However, he makes no comment about how Konrad truly died. Once again, mystery surrounded his death. It is obvious that there was a definite motive to kill Konrad. It's not a good idea to make enemies of rich people who are comfortable marching in the streets with swords, even if you do have a private army to protect yourself. How he died was important for me to find out. If he died peacefully in his bed or keeled over from a heart attack, it would mean that I did not share the same soul with him.

To be honest, I really wanted to have been Konrad—not because of the criminal aspect of his life but because he led men in exciting, unrestrained military battles, scheming against high-level enemies, and being able to act like a warlord, accountable to no one! Not to mention being at the very top of the food chain with all of the luxury that it brings. It must have been exhilarating. That life had to have been a lot of fun. Well, now, my curiosity had really been piqued. As I had access to the psychic world, I wanted to confirm that I was Konrad, but I needed to find out what had really happened to him.

Nanci Danison writes and says in her lectures that when one dies, his or her soul obtains universal knowledge. In other words, you know everything—past, present, and future. Since I have a limited ability to communicate with my deceased father, I try to tap into this source of knowledge through him occasionally. While my spiritual guides may not have wanted to share this information with me, I can always count on my loving father to be more indulgent. In my meditations, I asked my father if I had once been Konrad, and he confirmed it. I asked him if he knew what Konrad did, and Dad once again said yes. Yet despite my father's confirmation, I just would not be sure until Konrad's cause of death was revealed. Finally, I realized that there might be a way to find out what had happened to Konrad. I did belong to a group of talented psychics (myself excluded). I just needed a way to finagle a group reading to see if the psychics at the Mystic Nirvana could reconstruct the death scene, but I had to set it up in a way so that I would not influence their readings. As the Wicked Witch of the West once said, "These things have to be handled delicately."

I thought that the Thursday night psychic class at the Mystic Nirvana would be my best option to find out what happened to Konrad. The Thursday night class always has psychic exercises that Brenda leads. We had performed some of the exercises many times over the past months and I thought that I could offer a different exercise just to change the pace. I called Brenda and asked her if she would consider devoting a class to a CSI (crime scene investigation) exercise. But unlike *CSI: Miami*, we would not know if there had been a crime, and the events happened 750 years ago—a true cold case file. So I pitched the idea of the "CSI: Mystic Nirvana" class to Brenda, and she was agreeable to schedule it. On the Sunday night before the scheduled Thursday night class, I gave a sermon to the small Mystic Nirvana congregation. I taped Konrad's black cross coat of arms to the front of the lectern. With that, Konrad was once again restored to the pulpit! (Not that he made a habit of being in the pulpit much anyway.) A few people asked what the symbol was. I told them that it was the symbol of a powerful man who has a connection to the Mystic Nirvana and that this connection would be revealed at the Thursday night psychic class.

During that Thursday, I prepared small informational handouts that reprinted the Wikipedia history of Konrad so that the group would have a little background. Like a little kid at Christmas, I eagerly awaited the start of the 7:00 p.m. class. When I got there a few minutes before seven, I noticed that all the seats had been arranged in a large oval. I took a seat somewhere in the middle of the oval and waited for the festivities to begin. A fairly large crowd for a Thursday night settled in; all of the gifted psychics were there. Brenda stepped into the circle and then, unexpectedly, started to talk about her being attacked by malevolent spirits and saying that she wanted to teach us how to protect ourselves from them. (*What! What about the CSI exercise?* I mentally moaned.) Brenda did not give any details about who was attacking her or what they had done to her. This was the first I had heard about this kind of thing. Brenda insisted that we break into groups of four, and then she directed us to burn sage in each corner of the store. Finally, after the sage burning had scared away the bad spirits (I hadn't seen or felt any in the first place), we returned to the back meeting room to continue the class.

I got up to distribute my material, but Brenda sat me down and said that she couldn't devote the whole class time to my exercise. She then proceeded to hand out sealed envelopes containing pictures to everyone. (*Aww, man, what about my exercise?* I mentally whined.)

Brenda came up with a brand-new exercise in which everyone was supposed to take turns predicting what the sealed picture in their envelope was. This seemed to be more of an ESP exercise rather than a psychic exercise. Most of us were pretty good at revealing what someone would write in a sealed note, but we had never tried pictures before. *Okay, I'm game*, I thought. *Let's do this and move on to my exercise.* Everybody took turns predicting what their pictures were and everybody struck out miserably. Anybody who was even close received a lot of cheering from Brenda, but trust me, nobody was the slightest bit close. Well, after everybody had their turn, I figured it was time for my exercise. But no, Brenda insisted that the sealed picture exercise be repeated! (*Aww, man, you've got to be kidding me*, I thought. I was mentally whining like a little child at Christmas who was being denied his presents.) Now it was getting late in the class. The exercise was repeated with the same measure of success as the first round. I was dispirited because I thought that I would have to wait for another time, but then Laurie spoke up. "What about Frank's exercise?" With only fifteen minutes left in the class, Brenda allowed me to proceed.

I passed out my two-page handout with the second page containing a picture of the Konrad von Moontz photograph and the coat of arms. I gave a brief summary of Konrad's career and told the group that this ancient man was connected to our group in some way. I said that history books do not tell in any way how this man died on September 28, 1261—he may have died peacefully or he may have been killed. I asked the group to reconstruct his death scene and to tell me what his connection was to our group. There were about fifteen people seated in the oval, and Brenda had the lights out to make people more comfortable with their answers. The attendees were instructed to call out what they knew. Below are the readings of the individuals and my mental and verbal responses as I received them.

| Psychic | Reading | My Immediate Reaction |
|---------|---------|----------------------|
| Unknown | He was tired, in his bed chamber ready for sleep. | Hmm! |
| Bryan | Drunkard! Womanizer. | No surprise. |
| Bryan | Stabbed, killed | A-ha! |
| Laurie | He was gay. | Great. Just because *you* were gay in a past life does not mean everyone has to be. (Sorry, that was unbecoming of me.) |
| Unknown | Stabbed by someone he knew | A-ha! |
| Unknown | Power went to his head | Check. |
| Unknown | Blood, guts, it was an inside job | Comments are coming too fast to think. |
| Unknown Male | The first blow came from behind, struck him in the right ribs. | |
| Unknown | Yes, yes, there were four people stabbing him. It reminds me of the scene with Julius Caesar being stabbed by a group of men. | |
| Unknown | He was a pedophile! | What! |
| Laurie | That's right; he had a young teenage boy as a lover. | I blurted out, "No way!" |
| Unknown | It was a political killing. | |
| Unknown | The guards turned on him. | |
| Laurie | Yuck, the body was badly mutilated. | |

Finally, I had my victory. I discovered that Konrad had been stabbed and, therefore, that we very likely shared the same soul. This whole exercise was a validation from the spirits that I was, indeed, Konrad. However, I sat in my chair stunned at the revelation of the teenage male lover. *My alter-ego hero, Konrad—a pedophile*, I thought dejectedly. I then got up, thanked the group, and asked them what this man's connection to our group was. Most could not answer until, finally, Laurie said, "You were Konrad." Bryan then said, "I suspected as much." I sat down, disappointed, and Laurie approached me. "Don't be upset," she said. "The spirits want you to know that you are not the same man now as you once were. It's okay." I thanked her and said that I understood. And I did. However, my triumph in linking the true nature of Konrad's death to my soul was tarnished by the fact that Konrad would be considered a pedophile by today's standards. Ouch. (In ancient times, however, the practice was accepted.)

My best guess as to what happened to Konrad is that the fictional book almost had it right. The merchant families heavily bribed Konrad's secretary and his guards to kill him. He had incited a lot of anger, as evidenced by the fact that his body was mutilated after the murder. He was quickly wrapped in a death shroud and placed in a coffin. The next morning, the announcement was made that the beloved archbishop died in his sleep and went to his heavenly reward. Since he had been mutilated, there were certainly no public viewings of his body, and the secret of his death was maintained to this day. His (my) tomb is in the Cologne Cathedral's chapel of St. John. Not surprisingly, the imprisoned merchants escaped from their prison shortly thereafter.

If I may offer one comment in defense of Konrad, he was not all bad. He led the campaign to finance and start the construction of the famous Cologne Cathedral. He also ordained a priest who would later become known as Saint Thomas Aquinas.

Oh, one last thing. What was the lesson that my soul learned from the Konrad experience? That would be to not crave power over other people. I can remember remarking to myself many times in this life that I really avoid seeking power over other people. I guess I learned my lesson. However, I am still furious and warlike against my business rivals, and I am still full of tricks. Just ask my wife.

FOOTNOTES:

(1)    The anonymous writer who wrote the Reformatio
       Sigismundi in the 1440s had nothing but distaste for
       the belligerence of the German clergy. He wrote,

       Take a good look at how bishops act nowadays. They
       make war and cause unrest in the world; they behave
       like secular lords, which is of course what they are. And
       the money for this comes from pious donations that
       ought to go to honest parish work, and not spent on
       war … No bishop ought to own a castle. He ought to
       take up permanent residence in the principal church of
       his diocese and lead a spiritual life there. He should be
       an example to the clerics in his bishopric. But nowadays
       bishops ride about like lords in a secular state. Change
       this practice and you'll greatly increase the chances of
       peace.

(2)    Benjamin Arnold wrote about many German bishops
       and their war experiences. He made specific reference
       to Konrad when recounting the wars between cities and
       bishops.

       The city of Strasburg rose in defense of its rights
       against the new bishop Walter in 1261. When Walter
       campaigned against the townspeople, the bishop was
       defeated at the Battle of Hausbergen. Directing the
       battle in person, the bishop of Strasburg had two horses
       killed under him and reluctantly fled upon a third. More
       than 60 of his knights, including his brother and uncle,
       were killed and many more captured. In a struggle on
       a much larger scale, the political dispute which had
       originated in the 1150s between the archbishops of
       Cologne and the dukes of the lower Rhineland was
       finally resolved at the Battle of Worringen in 1288. A
       small but efficient Rhineland armed force destroyed
       Archbishop Siegfried's army, captured and imprisoned
       him for a year, and extorted a large ransom from him
       as well as his recognition of all their territorial rights.

No doubt Archbishops Walter and Siegfried were guilty of serious military misjudgments, but one of Siegfried's more formidable predecessors at Cologne, Konrad von Hochstaden, was different. Konrad was called "*vir furiosus et bellicosus*" (a man furious and warlike), and the annals of his time are full of praise for the aggressive tactics by which Konrad outfought his princely rivals in the archdiocese. One of his schemes was to introduce Earl Richard of Cornwall (the nephew of the famous English King, Richard the Lion Hearted) as holy Roman Emperor in 1257. The new emperor wrote home to his nephew, the Lord Edward, about the military campaigns in the Rhineland which his arrival had caused. He remarked with some enthusiasm: "Look what spirited and warlike archbishops we have in Germany; I would recommend that if you allowed the same in England, you would be secure against rebellion."

# Chapter 13: Guardian Angels and Their Tricks

*These things I warmly wish for you: someone to love, some work to do,*
*a bit o' sun, a bit o' cheer, and a guardian angel always near.*

— Irish blessing

## Reincarnation highway mile marker: USA, 2011

In 2011, Matt Damon starred in a movie called *The Adjustment Bureau*. The story focuses on a group of guardian angels who function behind the scenes to ensure that human lives stay on track with their cosmic plans. These guardian angels have an amazing array of powers to manipulate everyday objects to herd unsuspecting human beings back onto their planned tracks. They could interfere with telephones, spill coffee at the worst possible moment, cause accidents, and incite all kinds of other benevolent mayhem. Human beings think that the hidden actions of the guardian angels are only coincidences and mere chance events, but they are not. In the movie, the angels work very hard to ensure that Matt Damon's character, David Norris, does not marry his love interest because that event would ruin the individual life plans of both David and his lover. In the end, David becomes aware of the existence of the Adjustment Bureau and eventually overcomes the obstacles that they throw in his way. It's a fun movie, but its premise is actually closer to reality than fiction. The spirit world really does monitor your progress on earth and tries to guide you back if you veer too far off track. The guardian angels that perform this function are actually the spirit guides that Tony, the massage therapist, referred to previously. They are in no way as aggressive and interfering as the angels in the movie, but they do have many of the powers that the movie demonstrates.

Everyone on earth has at least one spiritual guide assigned to him or her, but nonpsychics do not know that they exist and are close by, ready to assist. Psychics, on the other hand, can readily sense and communicate with their guides. Those psychics who are lucky enough to have clairaudience receive regular spoken messages and advice. I have noticed that a sort of friendship develops between a psychic and his or her guide, in many cases. Since I am blind and deaf in the psychic world, I can't achieve that type of friendly relationship. But I do use my guide to connect to other spirits and to help me perform psychic readings in Brenda's class. One thing I did learn was that my guide's name is Mo, short for Morton. He spelled out the name when I asked for it in a meditation. Brenda added to my knowledge about him just after the hypnoregression session I told about in Chapter 7. She described seeing him laughing and engaged in an egg-throwing fight with another guide that was assigned to me named Gulliver. I thought then that it was only fitting that two jokers were assigned to my cosmic account. I really would not have it any other way.

My research in the psychic world turned up innumerable references to spirit guides. One story that resonates with this chapter is about a famous psychic who described how he first met his guide as a teenager. The guide came to him in a meditation and told him that he was there to assist him. To validate himself, the guide told the psychic that he was going to have a white rose delivered to his house. The next day, his older sister knocked on his the door carrying a white rose. The sister described some confusing circumstances in explaining how she came to have the rose, but she then handed it to him. The psychic was amazed, but he fully accepted his relationship with the guide from that point.

I, myself, have two funny personal stories to illustrate how the powers of guides come close to the abilities shown in the Matt Damon movie. The first story happened in the late winter of 2010.

I am not a Facebook or Twitter type of guy; I don't want to bore other people with details of my life or my latest thoughts. However, my Cleveland mentor and psychic friend, Linda, asked me to join LinkedIn and connect to her business network on that site. When Linda asks, I am happy to comply. Once I joined LinkedIn, I was also connected to all of Linda's associates. *Coincidence of coincidences*, one of Linda's clients was a woman (a girl, when I knew her) whom I knew from the grocery store and dated before I dated Michele. Her name is Kathy Poole, and she is one of my most favorite people in this life. I had lost touch with her for over twenty years, and I learned that she had remarried and recently moved back to Ohio. She e-mailed me to say hello and gave me her phone number so we could catch up. I called her and had a great time talking to her. During the conversation, she said something really surprising. She told me that she was still friends with Michele (yes, that Michele/Lana) and that she saw her and her husband in person once a year (another *coincidence*). What was funny is that she said that Michele would reminisce with her about me when they got together and that their husbands always interjected that they shouldn't get too excited because I would be fat and bald by now. I told Kathy that I was flattered that they remembered me but surprised that they would considering the very short time we had spent together so long ago. Anyway, at the end of the conversation, Kathy gave me Michele's married name and her e-mail address.

After giving it some thought, I wondered if Michele would feel any special spiritual connection to me since we had spent time together in a past life. Was there a faint memory? After all, Laurie had remembered me from a past life, and we had shared just a passing glance we shared. Michele/Lana actually spent time with me over two lives. As I am a curious cat, I really wanted to know. I sent her an e-mail in which I joked that I was not fat or bald and then briefly told her about my spiritual experiences. I asked her to, the next time she was in a quiet, contemplative moment, reach out and see if she felt anything about a prior connection.

To be honest, I never had any expectations that Michele would have any soul memories. If she did, she would have responded to my e-mail. But I never got a response. Who could blame her? After getting that crazy e-mail, any good Catholic woman would be thanking God that there were three states separating her from that maniac in Ohio. After a decent interval of time, I Googled her name and found her work number. It turns out that she was a librarian at St. Thomas Aquinas High School (another *coincidence*—Archbishop Konrad von Hochstaden ordained that saint). I called her work number and heard her voice on her voice mail greeting, but I didn't leave a message. I called about three more times over the next three days, but no one ever picked up the telephone. I was busy at the time, so calling Michele left my mind, and I quite honestly forgot about the whole thing. I was to be reminded about calling her in an unusual way.

Karol and I have a Chrysler van to haul the kids around in. One of the van's nice features is that it has satellite TV with kids' channels to keep the munchkins occupied while I listen to satellite radio on a separate channel. I like listening to alternative rock, but my wife also drives the van and changes the music channel to other stations. One weekday afternoon, I jumped into the van to run a short errand. I had just hit the road when the song "Michelle" by the Beatles started to play. I didn't pay it much attention until the next song came on. It was "Miracles" by Jefferson Starship. That had been Michele's and my song during our time together. This was just too much of a *coincidence*. By this time in my psychic development, I did not have to go into meditation to ask psychic questions; all I had to do was to ask a silent question in my mind and I would get an involuntary head shake answer. While I was driving, I silently asked, *Are you trying to get my attention?* Yes. *Are you telling me that this is the day that Michele will answer the telephone?* Yes.

When I got home, I dialed her work number, and she immediately picked up.

"Hello, Michele," I said. "It's me." She knew right away who I was.

We briefly caught each other up on our lives, and then I told her about how I had received information about our past-life connection. She seemed to enjoy the story as I gave her a truncated version of it. I asked her if she had any feelings about this connection, and she said that she did not have any memories or feelings about it. "That's okay," I said, and then I told her about the two songs played in sequence that caused me to call her. She thought that was funny and then told me that whenever the Billy Joel song "Only the Good Die Young" comes on, she always thinks of me. If you're not familiar with the song, it's about a guy who tries to seduce a good Catholic girl. The opening line is "Come out, Virginia, don't let me wait. You Catholic girls start much too late." I laughed, and then we said good-bye shortly after that because she had to get back to work.

The very next morning, I packed the kids into the van to take them to school. Satellite radio does not work until you pull out of the garage because that's when you can pick up the signal. As I backed into the driveway, the radio suddenly came to life, blaring, "Come out, Virginia, don't let me wait. You Catholic girls start much too late." I laughed out loud, and my daughter asked me what was so funny. "I'll tell you at another time," I said with a smile.

My second guide story occurred after a one-on-one business meeting. Karol and I opened a second business, an interactive art studio and store. We, of course, had to have a website created for the store, so we hired a developer, whose first name was Ken. One evening, I met with Ken to make some adjustments to the website. Ken has a sense of humor, so after we were done, we spent some time shooting the breeze in his office. He shared with me some details of his difficult childhood and the fact that he was a recovering alcoholic. It was a little too much information for me, but I did ask him if he meditated to help him with his addiction. He said yes. Nowadays, if a person tells me that he meditates, I always ask him if he gets any unusual messages. Obviously, I am looking for other psychics to compare notes with.

Ken responded that he did not get messages but would just know things. "What things?" I asked. He told me that, during meditations, he would ask a question and the answer would simply arrive in his mind.

"Pretty cool," I said. "What else can you do?"

"Well," he said, "my wife, Jill, is always freaked out about cash flow in our business. I don't worry about it, though, because when times are tight, all I have to do is ask for cash during my meditations and, sure enough, a day or two later a check will arrive in the mail. It has never failed me."

What Ken was making reference to is a process called manifesting. The belief or theory of manifesting is that your soul itself is so powerful that you can actually change the course of events or make things happen without the assistance of God or a spirit guide. The author Nancy Danison writes extensively about this power in her book *Backwards*, which is included in my reading list at the end of this book.)

"You know, Ken, that power is called manifesting," I said.

"Yes, I do know, and I believe I could manifest almost anything I wanted."

"Well, I doubt very much that you can manifest a naked Jennifer Aniston to come through that doorway," I said jokingly.

Ken thought for a few seconds and then reached into one of his desk drawers. He had just had a birthday, so he had a stack of birthday cards in that drawer. He grabbed the very first envelope on the stack and handed it to me. I extracted the card, and the image on the card was a naked Jennifer Aniston. The photo was from her Rachel days on *Friends*, and there she was, lying on her stomach with her buns exposed.

I laughed and said, "Nicely done." By this point in my journey, nothing surprised me. I knew that the "other side" had arranged that little trick. The question was, whose guide was responsible for it? My best guess at the time was that it was Ken's guide. That night, during my meditation session, I asked Morton if he had arranged for Jennifer to make her appearance. The answer was yes. Why? He's a joker like me, and it seemed that he wanted to help with this book.

I could imagine that you might think that personal guides are only there for fun and games. I am sure that it sounds pretty comforting to know that you always have a guardian angel or spirit guide actively watching your back. However, there is another side to that coin. I am now going to share one of the most important spiritual lessons that I learned from this journey. In order to help with your spiritual growth, spirit guides can also arrange for a lot of pain to come to you. It's not that they're mean or vindictive, but rather it's your soul that asked that they provide experiences of bad things for growth purposes. As easy as it was to arrange the delivery of a naked picture of Jennifer Aniston, it is just as easy to deliver something painful. It turns out that your guide is loyal only to your soul, not your human body. There is a big difference between the two. A human being always wants some form of pleasure and good times, but souls want challenges to conquer that will make them stronger and better. Challenges can take the form of oppression, abuse, physical pain, illness, and anything else you can imagine. The bigger the obstacle that is conquered, the more the soul evolves. Evolving as a soul moves the soul closer to God, the whole point of this cosmic game. I know that this concept is radical and difficult to follow. However, it perfectly explains the thorny paradox of a God who allows pain to exist. It turns out that bad experiences are not God's fault; you asked for them.

To provide a good illustration of a soul asking for abuse in a lifetime, consider this one case study from the book *Your Soul's Plan*. The author, Robert Schwartz, uses a team of very talented psychics to recover case subjects' events and times in heaven before they started their lives on earth. This prebirth time is used by all souls (yes, reader, you too) to plan obstacles that are fine-tailored to help them reach their goals and improve in certain areas.

This one story goes as follows: Jon is a gay man who grew up in Alabama in the 1960s. His family was Baptist, and his town was very conservative. You can just imagine how miserable his childhood was under that scenario. He was abused unmercifully by his classmates for being different. Page 51 of the book recounts how his classmates "were impressed (encouraged) by their guides to say (cruel) things. Their guides were working in concert with Jon's spiritual guide. There were given phrases, nasty things to blurt out." Schwartz stated that he had been surprised by this revelation. He had not heard that spirit guides could influence people in their speech. Nevertheless, this information was consistent with that received in other sessions where Schwartz learned that our guides work diligently to ensure that we have the experiences that we planned before birth, even when those experiences are painful. Though perhaps unpleasant or difficult to comprehend when viewed from the perspective of the human, this idea takes on an entirely different meaning when considered from the viewpoint of the soul. As souls, we know that life is a drama on the earthly stage and that our souls will be harmed by them no more than an actor can be harmed by another actor's lines.

I tell the story of Jon because it helps explain some of the difficulties of my current life. If you remember from Chapter 6 of this book, the spirit of my deceased father told me, "I now know that you had difficult times in your teen years." The word *difficult* was an understatement. I had never breathed a word of my difficulties to my father when he was alive, but he learned about them in the afterlife. I would eventually use the services of one of the psychics that Robert Schwartz used to uncover the spiritual meaning of my own "difficult times" and how my violent past lives were connected to my current one.

# Chapter 14: Gorman and Zul

*He paid the ultimate price, and I can never forget his sacrifice.*
— Robert A. Brady

## Reincarnation highway mile marker: Scotland, eighth century, and Germany, eighteenth century

It was a little while after I discovered that I had once been Archbishop Konrad that I went on a short business trip to Cincinnati with my junior partners Terri and Renee, the managers of our business in Cleveland and married women with children. The normal procedure for joint trips was for them to drive down from Cleveland so that we could travel together. Our appointment in Cincinnati was successful, so in celebration, I offered to buy a reading from Brenda for the both of them before they went back to Cleveland. The reason my offer came to my mind was that we would be passing the Mystic Nirvana on the way back from our business appointment. My goal was just to have some fun, but I did not know how they would react to my offer as they were both committed Christians. Happily, both were up for the adventure. I called Brenda from the road, and fortuitously, she had an opening that fit our driving plans perfectly. The three of us walked into the Mystic Nirvana, and I introduced my two colleagues to Brenda, telling her that we would all be together in this reading but that it was really for Terri and Renee. I was just going to observe. We all squeezed into her office, and Brenda started. Although we could not see them, a small group of spirits congregated in Brenda's office, trying to pass messages to my colleagues. It was funny watching Brenda try to keep the messages straight between the two ladies. Eventually, it was established that Renee's grandmother, Rose, had come to visit, and Renee was very touched by the experience.

As the reading concluded, Brenda turned to me and said, "The other side told me that you have been taking long walks." That comment surprised me, but it was true. I had gotten into the habit of walking Bo-Bo, the wonder dog, on a big circuit around our neighborhood. I thought, *Uh-oh, someone's been watching me.* I didn't say anything more about it to Brenda at that time.

The next day, I thought about the long walk comment again. I had learned that when the other side says something, there's always a reason behind it. I thought I should make the effort to find out just who had been watching me. I called Brenda and made an appointment for next day. When we met, I sat down in her office and asked her a simple question. "Okay, Brenda, who is watching me on my long walks? Is it my World War II buddies?"

After a little bit of contemplation, she replied, "No, I see a man dressed in a plaid kilt, sitting on a branch of one of the trees in your backyard. He's watching you walk by on the sidewalk."

"Who is he? Does he know me?" I asked.

"Yes, his name is Zul. He was your brother-in-law. You were married to his sister. I see her with long red hair. You had children with her."

"What is his interest in me?"

"You saved his life once," Brenda explained. "He came back to see how you're doing."

"How did I save his life and when?" I asked.

"Spirit is telling me it was in the late 700s. Your name was Gorman then. You lived in a Scottish village. I see you wearing a kilt. I see these big men—you know, the kind that wear those horns on their helmets?" Brenda is not the best with history. She was describing Vikings. She continued, "They are invading your village. You and Zul and some other men are trying to defend your village against them. I see you carrying a shield. Zul is fighting right next to you, and for some reason, he falls down. You move over to him and hold your shield high to defend him. By moving your shield up, you expose your belly to another Viking. He swings his axe and cuts you wide open. You go down, but Zul somehow escapes."

*Great*, I thought, *another bloody death! Well, at least I wasn't the aggressor this time. I was defending my family.* Then another thought hit me. It was really amazing that Zul would come down and look in on me after all these years. We must have been close. That thought was followed by angry ones. *Damn Vikings! To invade an innocent, hard-working village just to steal, kill, and rape. They killed me, and God knows what happened to my wife that day and afterward. How would she survive with me dead? Those Vikings were scum! What right did they have to do that?* My thoughts about what happened to my old village sound righteously indignant, don't they? Well, there's an old saying that people who live in glass houses should not throw stones.

Just as I was adding the life of Gorman to my collection of past lives, I stumbled upon another one. During one of my meditations in the fall of 2010, a hazy description of another fatal military life was revealed to me, this one set in Germany in the 1700s. On a business trip to Cleveland, I went to a psychic up there just for fun. I didn't ask her about this new life, but I just asked her to pass on whatever information the other side wanted to give me. Adding to my recent revelation, she described a vision of me in a colorful blue uniform, not dissimilar to the style of the American Revolutionary War uniforms. She described me wearing this uniform, lying on a road bleeding to death from a gunshot wound to the back. That's all she had, so I knew that more information would come about this life in the future.

All of these bloody deaths were starting to get depressing. What are the positives about reincarnation when the process (at least for me) seems to be a violent version of the movie *Groundhog Day*? How many more of these lives were out there waiting to be discovered? More important, what did I do to deserve all of this?

# Chapter 15: My Spiritual Crisis and the Return of Shem

*God will not look you over for medals, degrees, or diplomas, but for scars.*

—Elbert Hubbard

*When God permits His children to go through the furnace, He keeps His eye on the clock and His hand on the thermostat. His loving heart knows how much and how long.*

—Warren Wiersbe

## Reincarnation highway mile marker: USA, 2011

Here's a funny question. What is a malady that atheists cannot have that religious people can? The answer is a spiritual crisis. If you do not believe in God, you cannot have a crisis about the topic. As an atheist, I had immunity to spiritual disorders, but then I found out that there is a higher power. Then events conspired to cause me to have just such a crisis. How did I know that the phrase *spiritual crisis* described what I was feeling? I simply assumed that the term was correct, but to double check, I looked up the definition on Wikipedia.

**Spiritual crisis** (also called "spiritual emergency") is a form of identity crisis where an individual experiences drastic changes to their meaning system (i.e., their unique purposes, goals, values, attitude and beliefs, identity, and focus) typically because of a spontaneous spiritual experience. A spiritual crisis may cause significant disruption in psychological, social, and occupational functioning. Among the spiritual experiences thought to lead to episodes of spiritual crisis or spiritual emergency are psychiatric complications related to mystical experience, near-death experiences, paranormal experiences, religious ecstasy, and meditation or other spiritual practices.

Yup, that definition fit me to the proverbial T. What were my symptoms? I became emotionally upset because I could not reconcile how a loving God would allow me to have so many bloody, violent deaths. To this point, all of the revelations of my past lives did not indicate that I had any happy lives or joy. There were no stories of my doing good deeds in this world or making a positive difference and no stories of great, romantic loves. There were no feel-good stories—none whatsoever. In my life as Frank, I had always thought of myself as a decent person, one who was respectful of others and did not want to cause anyone pain. So why were there no revelations of past *good* lives to reflect my positive aspects? Why was I hearing only about the bad? What is the advantage of reincarnation if the process is a never-ending treadmill of violent death and bad times?

Compounding these feelings were feelings of grief that came to me when I was dreaming. Tony had previously talked about energy imprints from prior lives and how they could store emotions that could be released in a present life. I thought that, if I had any within me, they were starting to leak. During my childhood, I had the reputation of a boy who never cried. One night, at the age of fifty-four, I woke up from a dream with a tear dripping down the side of my face. I could not remember the dream that I had just had, but I had this feeling that I was mourning my dead friends from the war. I could sense that some of them were still with me, closely watching what I do in this life. In the last life, I never had the opportunity to decompress after the losses; Otto was too busy trying to survive and then died suddenly. Now it was as if I had woken up and had to address that trauma. My mood changed to an underlying melancholy. How does one deal with such a strange sense of loss? Who would possibly understand?

All of this past-life trauma would be easier to handle if the joys of my current life could counterbalance my painful past. Unfortunately for me, that would not be the case. Don't get me wrong—I am tremendously grateful for what life bestowed upon me once I reached the age of fifty, but a long, consistently negative period in my younger life had tainted my viewpoint of this life. I can honestly say that if I was on my deathbed and was offered a magic pill that would allow me to relive my teens and twenties, I would, without hesitation, refuse to take it. What was so bad about that time period? I could only describe it as going through a gauntlet of social exclusion and ridicule.

It was not always that way in my youth. In contrast to my teens and twenties, the times between six and eleven years old were very happy. Although my family did not have much money then, I had a great group of friends in my neighborhood and enjoyed a long stretch of continuous good times. I felt very happy and positive about the world before I turned twelve. The change came at the start of junior high school. It was as if someone (the Adjustment Bureau?) turned off the happiness switch in my life and left it off for twenty years. *Poof!* Lights out on the good times, just like that. Overnight, it went from "Everybody likes me" to "Nobody wants me on their team." After my adolescence started, I noticed that I was starting to be excluded and had no real idea why. As a teenager, I was a decent-looking guy, but I was on the short and thin side. I was also a bit introverted and certainly not obnoxious or offensive. But society was dead set on assigning me to a lower order on the social scale. The problem was that I refused to accept this judgment. Internally, I never saw myself as smaller than average, and I expected an equal shot at things. In fact, for some silly reason, I expected more than the average, so I would push back and fight hard for the things I wanted. My younger life consisted of fighting to make two steps forward and then having society slam me back hard one step. When I would get slammed back, it was in the form of an embarrassment that would have crushed the self-esteem of a weaker person. But instead of being crushed, I would get back up and keep fighting.

I will spare you most of the gory details of that time period. Instead, I will use the analogy of my early adult life as two trains that carried the two most important things that I cherished at the time—romantic love and career. Both of these trains pulled out of life's train station on parallel tracks when I was twenty-one. Their mutual destination was the land of happiness, but those particular trains would never arrive at that destination.

The love train carried the experiences of losing my first girlfriend, Michele (a girlfriend in two lives), and having to be forced to painfully watch her be in a relationship with another guy at the store where we worked. Ouch! I then met my first wife at college, an absolutely beautiful girl named Julie. The problem with Julie was that I knew that we were not right for each other. She really did not treat me well when we dated. However, it seemed that, despite my best efforts to find someone kinder, Julie was the only girl that the universe would allow me to date in my twenties. After five years of dating, I knew that I should leave the relationship no matter how painful it would be for me. When I had the "good-bye for good" conversation with her, I knew that she could easily replace me in two days' time. But for some reason, she told me that she wanted to get engaged and that she promised to be a good partner. I then took a big, calculated risk. We married at the age of twenty-seven and bought a nice colonial house together. However, I quickly found that my initial instincts had been correct. Julie was never happy in our marriage, and she was not the partner that she promised to be. Why did she marry me in the first place? That's a spiritual question that we will explore later.

My career train also had a rough start. After graduating college, I was hired at Ohio Bell and then quickly fired after six weeks, when I was falsely accused of cheating on a training exam. It's a long story, but I did not have to cheat and I did not cheat. The experience was just another one of those weird coincidences during this dark age that created great personal embarrassment and pain. A few months later, I was hired at a large bank as an operations analyst. There, I developed a reputation as a good manager who could fix badly broken departments. The bank rewarded me with many promotions over eight years, but senior management had typecast me and would not move me into financial sales positions, where the lucrative compensation was. Frustrated with not being able to go where I wanted to, I took a big risk and became a stockbroker for a large brokerage firm in 1987. As soon as I joined that business, the hot stock market turned stone cold. Sales plummeted for everyone. Cold-calling prospective clients was an absolutely miserable, painful experience in that environment.

The stock market crash of 1987 was the pivotal event that caused my two speeding life trains to derail and collide in a spectacular, fiery crash. I was fired from the brokerage firm for not meeting my sales quota. What could I do? After the crash, no one was buying securities. Julie then lost complete interest in our marriage, and we became nothing more than roommates. But I could not leave her because the financial industry stopped hiring for a solid year. I needed a job to move out and start my life anew. After twelve miserable months of loneliness and unemployment, I took a management job at a social agency that allowed me to get an amicable divorce from Julie. I happily moved into a singles apartment, and eight months after our divorce, Julie remarried.

Unfortunately for me on the job front, the social workers in my new office somehow found out about the salary I was making there. (Believe me, it was not that big of a salary.) That led to a jealous revolution among the staff, and the owner had to let me go. *Wow! Unemployed again!*

That was the official low point of my life. I was unemployed, divorced, and living alone in an apartment with no apparent prospects. At least my apartment had free hot water; I remember taking endless hot showers and just sitting on the bathtub floor, trying to figure out how to get myself out of that mess.

Fortunately, just after touching rock bottom, someone suddenly turned the happiness switch back on in my life. A personnel recruiter placed me into one of the lucrative financial sales positions that I had always wanted in banking. I finally got an opportunity to date a lot of girls, and I was finally having fun again.

Five years after my divorce, I married Karol. Karol is a very loving person and a great partner, but life still was not all roses. We suffered the pain of miscarriages before we were blessed with our twins. Also, I mentioned in a previous chapter that we almost lost our prosperous business because of the actions of our state government. It took an incredible effort on our part to save our business via a five-year lawsuit. I hope that, now that I have shared this background, you can understand why I would not want to relive this life.

The combination of past-life war trauma, the revelations of only bloody past lives, and an unhappy current life mixed together to form an evil brew. What really brought them together was a strange observation that I made during a rainy drive to Cleveland. I remember coming up behind a particular semi in the right lane on the interstate. It was raining very hard, and semitrucks can kick up a lot of spray that's hard to see through. When I moved into the passing lane to get around the truck, I noticed that the trailer was designed to carry livestock. Inside it were tightly stacked metal cages filled with white chickens. The sides of the trailer had open slats so that air could get in, but the openness also allowed the cold, billowing spray from the truck's wheels to drench the poor chickens. As I started to pass the trailer, one particular chicken actually made eye contact with me. As we looked at each other, I saw that the chicken's feathers were wet and matted and that he looked absolutely miserable. I would have thought that the chicken would have his head down in an attempt to shield himself from the driving spray; instead, he held his head upright in a proud type of posture. Wherever that truck was going, I knew that my poor chicken friend was going to meet his end there. He was on his way to his demise, and he had to suffer this painful, humiliating experience on his last journey. A connection then came together in my mind. *I'm not much different than you, chicken! We both suffer painful indignities in life and then get a bloody end. God knows how many more times I have met an unpleasant end than have already been revealed to me. What am I, some kind of cosmic whipping boy? Did my sins as Konrad require that I suffer so much?* In my readings of my spiritual books, one common theme was repeated—if you come down to earth to live a life, you volunteered for it. It was and is a matter of free choice for all individuals. With the mood that I was in at the time, I made a decision. I thought, *That's it. This sucks so bad down here that I am not coming back again!* I decided then and there to never return to earth in a body again!

Well, I had certainly progressed a long way spiritually, from gratefully discovering that humans do escape the finality of death (through reincarnation) to then trying to avoid the whole process entirely. Part of me felt like I was being an ingrate for thinking such thoughts. However, after having made my decision, I felt much better. I resolved to enjoy the rest of my life, knowing that this would be my last go-round. However, the other side would have a few comments about my decision.

The first comment came from Nancy Danison, the author of the book *Backwards*. During a medical procedure, Danison had a near-death experience that transported her into the afterlife, and she returned with memories of what she learned there. These memories serve as the basis of her book, which I highly recommend. You might think that she is a new-age lightweight, but think again. When she died during the medical procedure, she was a law partner at a major law firm. Brenda had Danison speak to us one night at the Mystic Nirvana, where she gave a fascinating talk and then took questions. When it was my turn to ask a question, I made a comment instead. I told her that I admired that she was able to overcome the temptation to stay in heaven. I then remarked that I would not have her courage because I am not going to come back to Earth again. Nancy smiled and said, "Well, the grass is always greener on the other side." That comment would stick in my mind—what was I missing?

The second series of comments came from my spirit teacher—Shem, the Native American chief. Brenda announced that Shem would be making another appearance through Greg. I found the prospect very exciting and told a number of people that they really should not miss an opportunity to see this. On the Sunday night that Greg was going to channel Shem, I got a babysitter to watch the kids and brought Karol to witness the event. I also brought my notebook because I had a whole new series of questions for him.

The Mystic Nirvana had a much bigger crowd than usual on the night that Shem made his second appearance. Greg went through his normal warm-up routine, and then Shem entered his body. This time, Shem wanted to talk face to face with whomever was going to ask him questions. I was fortunate enough to be the first one to sit in front of him. Previously, I had made contact with Shem in my meditations at home and asked him questions, and I wanted to be sure that it was really Shem I was communicating with. I asked, "Did we connect in my meditations?" And Shem replied, "Yes."

Before I had my chance to ask questions, I overheard something interesting when someone else brought up the subject of spirit guides. Shem said that the concept of spirit guides was really a human concept and that if you want to seek guidance, you should really go directly to God. That perked my ears up—talk directly to God? That's a scary concept, especially to someone from a distant Catholic background. Catholics always had the saints intercede on their behalf with God. To speak directly to the Godhead seemed almost blasphemous. I followed up on this subject with Shem.

"You mean it's okay to talk to God and ask direct questions?" I said. He replied, "Of course. There is no separation between you and God. Do not use guides; talk directly to the Great Spirit."

I turned and looked at Brenda for confirmation of this fantastic concept. She immediately affirmed what Shem had said.

Then things took a turn for the worst. I ended up in a verbal fight with a ghost.

"In my meditations," I began, "I am still told that I never was a woman in any of my lives, but you say that I was. How do I reconcile this information?" Shem asked, "Who are you talking to?" "My guides," I replied. Then Shem, in an exasperated, loud voice, said, "You are not talking to spirit guides; you are talking to low spirits!" Low spirits are ghosts who do not enter the white light upon their death and do not immediately return to heaven. They choose to remain "outside" the established system, causing mischief and haunting places. Shem appeared to hold these spirits in low regard.

I asked, "How should I know? I cannot see or hear who I am contacting." (He's chastising me as if I did not read the manual on being a psychic, except there is no manual and no guidance.)

"You do not communicate correctly at all," he said. (Once again he was criticizing my psychic communication system, just like last time. I am starting to get angry because he was berating me about something I have no control over. I would like nothing better than to be clairvoyant or clairaudient, I just did not receive those gifts despite my best efforts.

I said, "This is all that is given to me; I do not have control over this. (I was getting more frustrated and angry with his attitude.) And let me tell you something else, I am sick of being killed down here. I am not going back. This is my last life here!"

Shem, obviously very angry, replied, "You don't make that choice down here! That decision is only made on the other side!"

"Well, I am!" I said. "I have free choice, and I have had enough."

"You need to get right," he said, shaking his head in disgust.

You must realize that my emotional state was not in a good place at this time. I knew that Shem had once been a warrior, and I felt that he was not respecting me as a fellow ex-warrior. Shem talked about how we should be in touch with our hearts and our feelings, and I truly was then. I was feeling pain, but I felt that he was berating me and minimizing the depressing past lives that I had discovered. I wanted to call in the "you owe me respect as a fellow warrior" chip. To do so, I was going to use a Native American phrase that means "I kicked ass on my enemies.")

"Get it right, you say?" I said. "Listen, I counted coup on my enemies. You owe me respect." Angry and exasperated, Shem shot back, "And what does that have to do with this life?"

"Well, your side is sure making a big deal out of my warrior lives; just what *do* they have to do with this life? (I had just asked a crucial question, but it was not to be answered that night.)

Shem turned to Brenda and told her with exasperation, "You need to really help him."

Brenda just smiled and nodded her head. Karol watched all of this in utter amazement and was highly amused. I got up and stomped back to my chair. Greg woke up later, none the wiser to my little confrontation with the foreign spirit that had been in his body. That was the last time I ever encountered Shem. In retrospect, he was an important teacher to me, and I am very grateful for my time with him, even though he was a bit tough on me.

A few days later, during one of my nightly meditations before bed, I got information about another young soldier that I was once responsible for. His name was Hans, not to be confused with the first Hans, who had been killed by a sniper. After my death, this Hans had fought on and survived the Kurland Peninsula siege. He then went into Russian captivity and perished in a prison camp, never to come home. My sadness increased. I told Karol about this experience at the kitchen counter the next day, and tears rolled down my cheeks as I told her the story, very peculiar behavior for me, to say the least. Karol hugged me and said that she could tell that I was in real distress. She suggested that maybe I should talk to a counselor about it.

"Oh, yeah," I said. "I'll just tell the counselor that I am suffering from post-traumatic stress syndrome from World War II. I think that as a health professional, he would strongly recommend that I be committed."

But the more that I thought about it, the more I thought that maybe it was a good idea to talk to a counselor. However, it would have to be someone who could really address past-life issues. Where would I find someone like that? As usual, all I had to do was ask, and then the universe would provide.

To locate someone who could help me, my thinking was I would need a combination of a psychic and a counselor. I searched on the Internet for local psychics who specialized in past-life readings and found one who had a website that described her abilities; she did mention past-life counseling. I called her and told her about my problem and what I was looking for. She said that she was not the right person for me but that, for cases like mine, she recommended that I made an appointment to see Shellie Pate. Shellie Pate is a counselor who specialized in past-life trauma. (Who would believe that there were professionals that actually provided that kind of counseling?) I thanked her and then called Shellie. I told her about my issue, and she agreed to see me. I should not have been surprised when I found out that her office was within walking distance of my house. Isn't it amazing how these things worked out for me?

In the days before my appointment with Shellie, I did my own thinking about what was bothering me. My issues were as follows:

1. I hated my young adulthood.
2. I was grieving the loss of war comrades.
3. My exposure to multiple bloody past-life deaths was disturbing me. What was the meaning of these deaths, and what did they have to do with me in this life?

As I thought about these issues, I made progress on issues one and two. As far as my lost comrades, I realized that we had all died painfully. However, most of my comrades were still in heaven, and I was the one stuck down here. There really was no reason to feel sorry for my old comrades. As the ghost of Professor Dumbledore said to Harry Potter in the last movie, "Don't pity the dead, Harry. Pity the living." This line of thinking put my mind at ease.

As far as my young adulthood, I remembered the story of the gay man, Jon, that I relayed in Chapter 13. Jon chose a life of opposites to experience another point of view. In my life as Otto, I was five foot eleven inches and built like a strong farm boy. In my prior warrior lives, logic would say that I had to be larger in stature. In older times, you had to be big and imposing to be a soldier. This led to a realization in my mind that I must have requested an opposite lifetime plan as Frank. Such a plan would allow me to see the other side of being smaller and then give me the challenge of overcoming obstacles without using my brawn. It was an interesting theory that I had come up with, but what would counselor Shellie say?

By the time I met with Shellie, I was already feeling better emotionally. When I sat down with her and gave her my story and then my theory, she remarked that I had already done a lot of work on this issue. I did not take good notes and so cannot recount exactly all that she said. She did however say something profound and that was, "You are an alpha male who is extremely frustrated that you can't be an alpha male in this life." Her words hit me like a bolt of lightning. She had it exactly right! Those were my feelings exactly. No wonder this life felt so uncomfortable for me—it was because it was so foreign to me. I was forced to use only my wits when my instincts told me to knock people around. But that option was not available to Frank.

At the end of my appointment, I thanked Shellie for her efforts and never had to go back and see her again. I really did feel better as I was beginning to grasp what my life was all about. My primary goal now was to find the reason for all of my bloody past-life deaths.

Some important tools in trying to find this reason were the questions that I would ask in meditation. However, Shem's advice had changed to whom I was going to direct those questions. Going forward, I did start to follow Shem's advice to communicate directly with God or the Source rather than my guides. I was very tentative in the beginning but grew more comfortable as time went on. As my comfort level grew, I learned a very interesting thing about the Source. All spirits do not have genders because they do not have bodies. However, traditional Western culture has always considered God to be a male. I was curious about how the Source saw him- or herself, so I asked during one meditation session.

*What gender do you mostly identify with? Male?* I asked. No. *Female?* Yes. "Is it okay for me to refer to you as a female?" Yes. "Are you a low spirit?" I asked. (I had to be sure.) No. *Are you the creator of heaven and earth and the source of all consciousness?* I asked. Yes.

"Yes, ma'am!" I responded.

# Chapter 16: Time? What Time?

*My time is now.* —John Turner

## Reincarnation highway mile marker: Rest stop

Imagine driving your car eighty miles per hour down the interstate and wanting to program your GPS for the very first time. Obviously, you would not want to read the instruction manual while you were driving. Besides being dangerous, you would miss out on all of the sights that were speeding by your windshield. In this chapter, we are going to pull off of the reincarnation highway and take a brief moment to read some directions. We are doing this now because the highway is going to turn into a high-speed freeway after this chapter. We will not have time to stop and explain things then. At this rest stop, I want to provide context and background for some of the unusual things we are going to encounter.

Down the road we will meet a psychic with a client who had lived over more than one hundred lives just to master one life lesson. A hundred lives! Take a minute and ponder the idea of living 100 lives. All you math majors out there would almost immediately compute that a hundred lives multiplied by fifty years equals five thousand years! And if you add in a reasonable 20 year break between lives, that would stretch the consumption of time to 7,000 years. Going back 7,000 years would take you back well into pre-history and a dreary life of basic subsistence living. That would equate to living centuries of lives as an almost cave man. I don't know about you, but I think two or three of those lives would be my limit. Doctor Newton's regression studies show that souls actually choose the lives that they want to live. How can you have absolute freedom of choice where and when you live your lives when there is a finite amount of available time? For example, suppose a soul wanted to restrict his (or her) lives to the more modern time span of 3,000 years where history was actually recorded and saved in some form. How would that soul do that if he needed 7,000 years to live a hundred lives? It sounds like an unsolvable paradox, but it is not because of a fact that you will have a very hard time grasping. That fact is that there really is no such thing as time in the spirit world. Past, present, and future exist at the same moment when you are in spirit form. With this strange little quirk in the universe, all souls can choose a new life anywhere on earth and during any time period that they want to experience. Therefore, you have an almost infinite number of opportunities to experience the lives you need to learn from. Living a hundred lives would be child's play in this "no time" system.

Nonsense, preposterous, and not supported by science, you say? Try again. Google the phrase "Does time exist?" and you will get 137 million results. For example, on June 22, 2011, Morgan Freeman hosted an hour-long show called *Through the Wormhole: Does Time Exist?* You can watch it on the web; it's pretty interesting. The show revealed that cutting-edge physics cannot actually account for time.

The science of physics is revealing many dimensions of reality that we, as humans, do not sense. One of these unseen dimensions is the true nature of time. This was actually revealed when Einstein's special and general theories of relativity destroyed the idea that time was a universal constant. The fallout from this theory was the realization that the past, present, and future are not absolutes. Even more interesting results occur when physicists try to reconcile Einstein's theory of relativity with quantum mechanics. The Wheeler-DeWitt equation was the result of one attempt to bring these two theories together.

An article in the June 2007 issue of *Discover* Magazine entitled "Newsflash: Time May Not Exist" expands on the outcome of this effort as far as the true nature of time.

> Einstein's theories also opened a rift in physics because the rules of general relativity (which describe gravity and the large-scale structure of the cosmos) seem incompatible with those of quantum physics (which govern the realm of the tiny). "One finds that time just disappears from the Wheeler-DeWitt

equation," says Carlo Rovelli, a physicist at the University of the Mediterranean in Marseille, France. It may be that the best way to think about quantum reality is to give up the notion of time—that the fundamental description of the universe must be timeless."

Adding to this idea, Robert Lanza stated in a spring 2007 essay in *The American Scholar* that "Einstein was frustrated by the threat of quantum uncertainty to the hypothesis he called spacetime, and spacetime turned out to be incompatible with the world discovered by quantum physics. When Einstein showed that there is no universal now (meaning no universal present time), it followed that observers could slice up reality into past, present, and future in different ways, all with equal reality."

I am not going to go too deep into the "does time exist" debate. You can research it for yourself. My only goal in discussing this physics theory is to show that, if it is true, it would allow for multiple lives anywhere and anytime you choose. As a matter of fact, the concept of "no time" neatly explains how some supernatural psychic events can occur. For example, let me tell you a story that only the concept of there being no time would explain.

I have had a number of readings from Brenda. I always took notes so that I could go back and refer to them. During one reading, Brenda asked me if my daughter Jani had her own bathroom on our lower level. I responded yes.

"You need to get her toilet checked," she said. "I see a water explosion with sewage flowing all over the floor!"

"When is this going to happen?" I asked.

"I don't know. I just see it happening," answered Brenda.

When I got home later, I flushed Jani's toilet to see if there was a problem. It ran just fine, and I quickly forgot about Brenda's vision. I know Karol would have called a plumber, but I didn't. A little over a year later, my mother-in-law was staying with us overnight and went to use Jani's bathroom. I was watching TV upstairs when I heard yelling and screaming downstairs. Jani's toilet was flooding, and—you guessed it—there was sewage was all over the floor. My elderly mother-in-law was horrified as she was stranded in the bathroom with a current of water rushing out the door and into the hallway. Thank God, the hallway outside that bathroom is tile rather than carpet! I immediately remembered Brenda's prediction as I rushed to clean up the god-awful mess. The problem was serious enough that it required a plumber to fix. I know this is a funny story, but it has a profound question hiding in it—how did Brenda know that this was going to happen? It happened at least fourteen months after Brenda had her vision. How can psychics sometimes see the future? The answer is that there is no time. The past, present, and future are one in the spirit world. Brenda tapped into the spiritual world and saw that messy event in the future as easily as she can see me in a past life.

So if spirits know the past, present, and future, why do we experience time as humans? Good question. The answer is that time is used to enhance our earth visit by allowing us to experience something that is not available in the spirit world—surprise. Think about it. If you knew the future, you could never be surprised by any event. Nanci Danison best describes this whole concept in her book *Backwards*.

> The simple potential of the unknown thrills us in our role as souls, for in our natural state all is known. Here, in human form, we can savor the deliciousness of the unknown. We are free on earth to go about our daily lives in complete and utter ignorance of what lies ahead. The physical limitations of the human brain block out our universal perspective and prevent us from seeing in advance the ramifications of all possible choices. You and I are forced by circumstances to choose rather blindly. And that is the whole point of being here! Where's the surprise if you know beforehand how events will turn out?

Danison's words are something to contemplate. If you comprehend what she is saying, you will have come a long way in understanding why we spend "time" on earth.

Going off on a tangent, here's another mystery that the "no time" concept will explain—that is, if you believe in ghosts. Let's start with a question. Why would ghosts (those pesky low spirits who temporarily get off of the reincarnation merry-go-round) haunt castles and houses for hundreds of years after they died? Wouldn't they grow tired fairly quickly of clunking up and down staircases? How could they stand doing that for centuries? The answer to that question is that once they leave their bodies, they no longer sense time. Two hundred years feels like twenty minutes to them. You've never looked at something that way before, have you? But it fits. It's an interesting concept to ponder.

I need you to take away one main concept from this chapter before we pull back onto the highway. Remember that since past, present, and future occur at the same time in the spirit world, an event that happens in the future on earth can actually affect an event that happened in the "past." In other words, don't get too hung up if historical things occur out of chronological order.

# Chapter 17: My Life as Frank Explained

*Basically, we are all looking for someone who knows who we are and will break it to us gently.*

—Robert Brault

## Reincarnation highway mile marker: USA, 2012

In Chapter 15, I described how I had received strong indications that my soul purposely planned the life of Frank, a life that I would absolutely refuse to live again. My incarnation before Frank was a young German soldier named Otto. If my theory is correct, my soul was in the personality of Otto when my life as Frank was designed. My simple question became, "What was he thinking?" After enduring the trauma of World War II, you would think that Otto would cut himself a break and design a much more fun life. Then again, maybe it's only a matter of perspective. It can be truthfully said that nobody has ever shot at me as Frank, nor have I ever been hungry or cold without an opportunity for warmth in this life. And I have always had access to hot water. Compared to Otto's life, my life was a cake walk. Still, I really wanted to know why my life had been designed as it was. Why did the personality of Frank specifically come after Otto? How was Frank some kind of progression or evolution over Otto? To find out this information, I would have to go to a specialist.

As I mentioned previously, the book *Your Soul's Plan* centers on exploring prelife planning by using a group of very talented psychics who work with the book's case subjects to uncover their prelife planning processes. Just as important, the book explores *why* they planned their lives the way that they did. This type of revelation was exactly what I wanted. Of all the psychics in *Your Soul's Plan*, I admired the work of Staci Wells the most. I decided then to track her down and try to arrange my own reading with her.

I found that she has her own website on which people can book their very own readings. Staci lives in Arizona, but seeing her (or any psychic) in person is not a requirement. Readings can be conducted through a long telephone call. Using her website's automated booking feature, I signed right up for an appointment. Because of *Your Soul's Plan,* she is very popular and in high demand, and the earliest available appointment was three weeks out. When I made the appointment, I sent the below e-mail to Staci to introduce myself and my goals:

Hello, Staci. My name is Frank Mares from Powell, Ohio. I am a clairsentient psychic who has been doing a lot of work with other Columbus-area psychics to flesh out the details of my past lives. It would be very helpful to me to now use your services to see how the traumatic events in my past lives tie into my current life. As Robert Schwartz might say in his books, I have had a full life in that I had a lot of hard challenges thrown at me. I prevailed against tough odds, but I want to know why I had to go through these "trials of fire." I read about your great work in *Your Soul's Plan*, and I think you could help me greatly. I look forward to working with you.

A few days before my reading, I asked the Source during my nightly meditation if she had any messages or insight for me. I ask this question almost every day, and most times the answer is no. On this day, I got a yes through my involuntary nodding. The message I got was a cryptic "jackbooting through the" with no noun to tell me what I would be jackbooting through. Despite my best efforts, I could not get any hint at the last word in the sentence. I was being spoon-fed again. (For those who do not know, jackboots are what the German soldiers wore in both World Wars but especially in the second. The term "to jackboot" implies that the wearer is aggressively marching somewhere to take it over.) In frustration, I asked the Source if I should ask Staci Wells to complete the sentence, and the Source responded yes with a head shake.

After a three-week wait, my reading day with Staci arrived. At 2:00 p.m. on a weekday afternoon, I called her number and was greeted by a friendly, warm voice. Staci normally allocates ninety minutes for a life-planning reading, but as it turned out, she had so much material for me that the appointment actually lasted two hours! All I can say is that I received everything I had expected and more. As a matter of normal procedure, Staci tapes her readings with her clients and then sends them an MP3 recording of it. This was extremely fortunate because now I have the exact transcripts to share with you. However, to make things concise and better flowing, I have edited and reorganized the content.

Staci started our session by saying that, for my reading, she had more notes to refer to than usual. These notes had come from her meditations when she asked for and received information about me. Her opening counsel was that, when looking at all of the lives that a soul chooses to live, each life should be considered a brushstroke of what the soul wants to be.

She then gave me a most valuable gift. Without my mentioning or even hinting at its existence, she explained the reason for the youthful pain that I recounted two chapters ago. She revealed that my life plan was set to have the first thirty to thirty-three years be an "extensive, extended experience of frustration where I would not get affirmation from others." (Oh, my God! She had scored a bull's-eye!) Remember that I said that my happiness switch was turned off at age twelve and was not to be turned on again until I was thirty-three? I also felt that, other than my family, no one thought I was worth a damn. I had always felt that the world was conspiring against me then, and here she had just confirmed it!

"How could such a frustrating experience be arranged?" I asked. She replied, "Before you came down here, you entered into soul agreements with others to make your life miserable during that time frame."

"Why would I inflict so much pain on myself?"

Staci explained that most souls choose to work on three to five karmic lessons in a given lifetime and that lesson choices vary from lifetime to lifetime. Each lifetime is specifically planned to give the soul the opportunity to address the lessons it chose to work on. She then revealed to me that I had chosen to work on four specific lessons. I asked, "Which lesson was responsible for the pain in my youth?" "The second-hardest lesson of all to learn," she answered. "That is the lesson of self-esteem and self-worth."

After later reflection, that made perfect sense. Every incident outlined in Chapter 15 (and there were many more that I did not include) was perfectly designed to crush my self-esteem. That period was a constant attack on my self-worth, but through it all, I never faltered. I never stopped believing in myself, and I always got back up when I was knocked down.

"What other lessons did I choose?"

Staci replied, "You also chose the lessons of emotional independence, learning at a core level that you are your only true source of happiness and well-being and that you cannot rely on others for your happiness. Also, to be harmonious and to work cooperatively for the greater good and for beneficial relationships. And finally, the karmic lesson of balance and emotional flexibility—gaining strength from the emotional connection to your soul."

"Let's go back to the most painful one of self-esteem," I said. "Why that one?"

"You needed to learn that what others thought of you should not concern you. This all goes back to your prior lives. As a soul, you actually chose to go on the leadership track when you picked your lives. That is, you wanted lives in which you could lead others. If you were on the leadership track and then choose to work on the karmic lesson of self-worth and self-esteem, it's because you had made missteps in those prior lives. You allowed your emotional neediness to interfere with how you lead others. You did not lead them to their highest good. During your life reviews after you died, you realized that you must improve your emotional well-being at the soul level, that the only way you could progress was to get your emotional house in order. The Source is telling me that there were two lives in particular in which this happened. The Source said that your energy became disturbed."

*Uh-oh,* I thought. *There's a hidden, bad life out there whose existence is just being revealed to me. The spoon-feeding process is continuing, and another baby spoon of information was just fed to me by the other side through Staci.*

"Well, I certainly can see that the life of Archbishop Konrad was one of these lives," I said. "I definitely did not lead others to their higher good then."

"At least you are making progress in this life," Staci said. "You haven't taken out your broadsword and cut anybody in half!" (This was another clue about the newly revealed, bad life. If she was emphasizing broadswords, I knew that this unrevealed life must involve the use of swords and not in a good way.)

"I didn't get the opportunity for swordplay in this life," I replied, "but, you know, deep down, I really miss that kind of life."

"Of course you do," Staci said. "You like the physicality and the experience of battle. It's a major high for you, but it was time for you to move on from that lifestyle. In your past lives, you had a very strong reactive streak to what others would say about you."

"Historians did say that Konrad was both aggressive and furious," I offered.

"You just proved my point. You would always adopt the dictates of the church or the royal court to fight for. You would respond strongly whenever someone pulled at your heartstrings by physically attacking them. You firmly believed that right had the might and that might will always win out. Your belief system often backfired, and then you would lose your life."

"I just remembered," I said. "The Source asked that I give you a message to complete. The message was that I was always 'jackbooting through the,' and you need to fill in the blank."

"That would be 'jackbooting through the universe,'" she replied. "You are a 'spiritual warrior' who has always fought for your version of right and truth. The Source is telling me now that there were six lives in which you were an active spiritual warrior. But you did not use the personal filters that you do now in this life. You need to be less violent. In your life as Frank, you needed to resolve differences peacefully instead of swinging a sword or getting a gun. You needed to learn to be wiser and not to use aggression. A more natural way will come to you of being gentle and cooperative."

"The planning of my current life is finally starting to make sense to me now."

"The Source is telling me that you will understand this phrase: 'The strength of emotional independence is in your legs,'" Staci said.

(It took me months to understand this phrase because it was stated in spiritual, symbolic terms, which I am terrible at deciphering. However, the message meant that to have emotional independence from what others say about me, I must have a strong emotional foundation, as legs are the foundation of the body.)

"What else can you say about Frank and this life lesson?" I asked.

"Well, in a life where you choose the lesson of self-esteem and self-worth, it is common that your personality will come equipped with the traits of strong will and creativity."

"That fits," I said. "I have those attributes."

"Overall, I would say that this life was a call from your soul to build a better foundation of self-worth so that you could express yourself and your truth."

"You mentioned that I chose the second-hardest karmic lesson to work on," I said. "What is the hardest?"

"That would be learning to control impulsive tendencies," Staci replied. "I actually had one client who spent over a hundred lives trying to learn how to control impulsive tendencies."

Now everything tied together. I could see that I am changing the way I will live my future lives and that Frank is just the start of the new way. But what is now in store for me in the rest of my life as Frank? Staci did address my future.

"Your life had a jumping-off point at thirty-four years and will have another one at sixty," she said. "At both of these points, you will exhibit a greater self-confidence in a way that you have not been able to before. In the age period of thirty-four to sixty, you will be working on achieving a new balance, and this new balance will affect what you write, express, and do.

"From the age of fifty-two to the end your life will be a life review for you. You will adapt the lessons you learned in this life and become a man who can be counted upon—not waging a battle, but rather to be effective in the lives of others. You are now counting on yourself and others and now want others to count on you. You want to be the one that people will come to when they have a problem. You goal now is to become a wise old man."

"You mentioned that I came to earth to express my truth. What does that mean?" I asked.

"Spirituality is already strongly established in your soul. You have a desire to teach what you have learned. You came to earth with a message, and now you are getting ready to teach others this message. However, this time, you will teach without aggression or assertiveness and without getting killed."

"One last question, Staci," I said. "When do you think I will be able to stay longer on the 'other side'? I always seem to be rushing back down here in time to catch the next war."

"If you die in a moment of passion in battle, you carry it with you in death. You use that energy to come right back. Maybe this time you will give yourself the peace of mind to enjoy yourself on the other side rather than rushing back to the drawing board and planning a new life to get it right."

In reflecting on what Staci said, I came to the realization that this book is the vehicle for my message and my teaching. After all, time is running out in this life. What else could it be but this book? I have no other tricks up my sleeve. Did I always intend to write this book as a lesson to others? I wish I could say that I did, but the truth is that my reasons were initially much more self-serving. Somewhere in all of my readings of spiritual material and books, I read that if you wrote a book about spirituality to share with others, you would not have to return to earth again in another life. (And you know how much I have enjoyed this life!) A book about my experiences just might be the ticket off of this earth merry-go-round. To be sure, I needed to confirm this with the Source. In my meditations, I asked several times if this book option was true, and I always received an affirmative answer. I now realize that both the question and the answer are tricky. The true answer is that you are never forced to come back to earth. You can quit at any time. It is your soul that pushes to come back down here so that it can learn and better itself. Writing a spiritual book has nothing to do with my future return. I was given that affirmative answer so I would have the motivation to write this book, and by the time I found out the truth, the book was almost complete anyway!

Another mystery that Staci solved was why the beautiful but disinterested Julie surprisingly urged me to marry her when she could have easily replaced me, as she did later. Marrying me made no logical sense as she was not that happy in our long dating relationship. The spiritual answer was that we had made an agreement before we were born that we would marry and then she would put me through the wringer as a test of my self-esteem. There is absolutely no reason to be angry with her if my soul specifically asked her for that test. She only did what she had been asked to do. Knowing this type of life-planning information really shows the value of the gift that Staci gave me. She explained all of my life's mysteries and why they happened, allowing me to jettison the anger and bitterness that I once held on to.

After I wrote the draft of this chapter, I shared it with Karol to get her thoughts. She read it and insisted that I add another theme to it.

This theme would be based upon her comment, "Linda would always ask you, 'How have your spiritual experiences made you better in this life?' You need to get your head out of the 'other side' and give concrete examples of how you are a better person now!"

Karol actually wanted a complete chapter devoted to this topic, but I am not Mother Teresa. I have not done enough good works to fill a separate chapter. All I can say is that I have tried to become a more giving person, and Karol agrees that I have become much better in this area since starting this journey. I did volunteer at the food bank until I got too busy. However, I still make a generous contribution every month to that cause. I try to lend a hand to people when I can, although I still have to push myself. I can certainly say that this experience has made me completely nonjudgmental of other people. As long as they are not doing harm to others, I accept them as they are because I know there is another soul in that person's body, and that soul is wearing that body to pursue the person's own life lessons, which are entirely his or her own business and choice. While every soul is unique, no soul is truly more important than another.

# Chapter 18: To Be a Member, You Have to Remember!

*All your life you pretend to be someone else and it turns out that you were someone else pretending to be you.*
—Robert Brault

## Reincarnation highway mile marker: Germany, sixteenth and nineteenth centuries

After my Staci Wells reading, I was very motivated to learn about the second, wicked life that had been revealed to me. I intuitively felt that this mystery life held the key to learning why my prior lives were so bloody. Unfortunately for me, the spoon-feeding rule was still in effect. That is, the spirits were going to feed me information at their pace, not as quickly as I would have liked. I tried numerous times in meditation to pry out information about this life, but all I received in return were very sparse facts such as the following:

- It was a life in the 1500 or 1600s.
- The life took place in Germany.
- I was a nobleman.
- My name was Nicholas.

I asked, *What was my great sin in that life?* The only answer I received was that I had been a womanizer. I knew from that answer that I was being stonewalled. Many women believe that a womanizer deserves a ticket to hell, but I knew better—information was being withheld from me. By this point in my journey, I knew that things would eventually be revealed but that I would have to wait until Spirit was ready. In the meantime, my writing of this book came to a crashing halt because a major piece of the puzzle was waiting to be revealed. I set the writing aside and concentrated on helping Karol plan and build her new art studio. This book would have to wait until I obtained that missing puzzle piece. After a break of a few months, I actually got the sign from the other side to proceed with the book through a hilarious dream.

The world of dreams is where the spirit world and your consciousness occasionally interact. Sometimes messages from spirits are put into your dreams; however, you must be able to interpret the spirit symbolism to understand it. One night after Karol's studio had finally opened, I dreamt that the studio was still unfinished. In the dream, I met with the builder at the construction site to see what the delay was, and he complained that he could not finish the job because spirits kept digging holes in the cement floor of the studio. The builder then showed me a gaping hole in the floor. I told him that I needed to go talk to the spirits to see what the problem was, somehow knowing that the offending spirits were located on the second floor of a nearby warehouse. With an unidentified group of strangers, I went into the warehouse and up to the second floor. From the rafters above, the unseen spirits started to chant, "To be a member, you have to remember." The strangers freaked out and started to cower, but I remained standing and started to smile. I said loudly, "That's right—to be a member, you have to remember!" I started to shake my fist in unison with the spirits and chanted with them. I remember then waking up and laughing. *What a great dream, and so vivid*, I thought. And then it hit me that it had to have been a message dream.

I remained in bed and asked the Source if that dream had been a message, and I got an affirmative head shake yes. I then began to analyze the dream for its true meaning. I realized that the unfinished studio was representative of this book. It could not be completed because there was a hole to be filled in the story. The spirits in the rafters were telling me the solution to the problem with the chant, "To be a member, you have to remember." That translates into, "To be a member of the spiritual world, you have to remember your past lives." When I came to this conclusion, I asked the Source if I had the interpretation correct, and my head nodded. I then asked the Source if she was finally ready to release information about Nicholas, and once again, I received an affirmative answer. The next morning, I called Brenda and told her about my dream. She loved my recounting of it and agreed with my conclusion. I then made an appointment with her to finally find out about my past life as Nicholas.

When I met with Brenda in her office, we got right down to work. I told her that I was looking for a past life set in the 1600s, that my name had been Nicholas, and that I had been a nobleman. I finished my description by telling her that Nicholas had done something bad, probably at least as bad as what Konrad had done.

Brenda sat back in her office chair and closed her eyes to concentrate. In about thirty seconds, she started to describe me when I was Nicholas. "I see you sitting in a chair in a big tent. My goodness, you are a big man—linebacker sized. You are sitting there eating a chicken leg and laughing. You have this big, deep, loud laugh. At your feet is all of this loot that you and your men stole. You are rejoicing over the take. You have a wide face with light eyes. Your hair is dark brown, long and wavy. You also have a moustache and a beard. It's not a thick beard; you have some thin patches."

"Describe my clothes," I said. "Am I wearing something that looks like velvet? I am supposed to be a nobleman."

"No, your clothes look more like leather to me," she replied. "Definitely not velvet." She then became silent as she was listening to more information that was being relayed to her. "Spirit tells me that you led a group of pillagers. You stole and killed unnecessarily. You loved all the power that you had. You walked as if you were invincible. I see you now with your sword. There's an inscription on it; it was passed on to you from your father. It was an ancestral sword. You are very proud of your family name. Honor and family were everything to you. I see you now cutting notches into the hilt of your sword, one notch for every town conquered.

Brenda went quiet again as she gathered more information. "You had a reputation of being a great swordsman. Your men put you on a pedestal because of your swordsmanship and fighting ability. Nobody dared touch your sword, and nobody crossed you. I have this picture of you riding your horse like Genghis Khan. You were real intense."

"In my meditations, the only information I got was that I was a womanizer," I offered.

"I do see the most beautiful women of the town being led to your tent, but trust me, there was no seduction on your part. I am also getting that you had a younger brother. He's a higher-level cleric. He is also gay. You do not respect him because he is not interested in playing the part of a nobleman and he is dismissive of your family name. Your family name is everything to you."

"Can you get a last name for Nicholas so that I can research him?" I asked. "I got something like Putlinz, but nothing definitive."

After some thought, Brenda said, "It's hazy, but I cannot make out the last name. Maybe it's Putlinz, but I cannot be sure."

"How did I die?"

"I don't know," she replied. "I see a vision of you and your men being surrounded, and you are fighting for your lives. You could have been stabbed in the stomach, but I really cannot tell. You were in your late forties in this battle scene."

I sat back to process this revelation. There may have been another violent end to one of my lives. But worst of all, I was behaving just like those Vikings who I had condemned for their actions when I was on the other end of the sword (or axe, in Gorman's case). How in the world could I display this kind of evil behavior when I had experienced the other side for myself? Hadn't I learned anything from my life as Konrad or as Gorman? What happened in the time between Konrad and Nicholas? Did something happen to make me even more evil?

"It's just amazing that after Konrad, I got even worse," I said. "Can you tell me about the lives between Konrad and Nicholas?"

Brenda thought for a while and said, "After Konrad, your soul wanted a simple life. You were a fisherman with a fairly large boat in Germany. I think you also hauled some cargo in that boat. There was nothing too exciting in that life."

"What about after the fisherman?"

"I don't know much about the Catholic Church, but I see you again as a high-ranking cleric. I see you as a very old man being attended to by other men in robes. You are actually blind in your old age; your voice is very soft and slow. The men show you great reverence. I think you had some disputes with the local authorities. It turned out that you were poisoned so that someone else could succeed you. It seems like this scene is set in Italy and your name is Thaddeus. After this life, your next life is Nicholas."

Like Brenda said, she is unfamiliar with the Catholic hierarchy. In my own personal meditations, I found out that I was an abbot of a big Cistercian monastery at Kamp-Lintfort, Germany. If you see pictures of the monastery grounds at Kamp-Lintfort, you will see rolling hills and beautiful gardens. It looks like Italy, but it's really western Germany. In the fifteenth century, monasteries were the engines of industrial production, and they had both economic and political power. As an abbot, my power would have been almost as high as that of a bishop, and I would have had opportunities to get into disagreements with the secular political authorities, as Brenda alluded to. The important thing about this life was that I was a good Christian and a good leader of my flock. I led them to the higher good. I believe my devoutness as Thaddeus was represented in the story in Chapter 8 when I mimicked the position of a priest deep in prayer. The sign of benediction that I made immediately afterward reflected Archbishop Konrad, the other side of the coin.

*The monastery at Kamp-Lintfort, Germany, the home of Abbot Thaddeus. Photography by Raimond Spekking*

The reading with Brenda continued. "What life did I have after Nicholas?" I asked. "Sometime in the 1700s, I know that I was a Prussian soldier who got shot and killed. Do you have any details on that life?"

Brenda thought for a bit before answering. "You were one of those soldiers who rode horses (cavalry). You were in your early twenties.

I see you in a blue uniform, kind of like those our soldiers wore in the Revolutionary War. You were riding your horse alone on a road when you stumbled upon the enemy. You turned around to warn your comrades, but you were shot in the back and fell down to the road below. You quickly died."

"What was my name then?"

"Gustav," Brenda replied.

"Was my next life as Karl, the dairy farmer?" I asked.

"Yes, but there is more to that life than you think there was. I see you at a desk writing your name on documents. Besides being a farmer, you are also a city official. I sense that you are thinking dark thoughts and that you are plotting something. The documents you are signing are deeds for property. It seems like it's some kind of swindle. I think this will lead to your murder. That's all I can get about this life."

"Good grief, Brenda," I said. "It's amazing you associate with me at all! After Karl, I lived the life of Alfred, his grandson, who dies in World War I. Then I die as Otto in World War II. I have quite a history, haven't I?"

"This is true," she said.

"Any idea how I could be so good as Thaddeus and then plunge into the depths of evil as Nicholas?" I asked.

"Like I said before, sometimes you are the persecuted and sometimes the persecutor."

"One last thing. Staci Wells said that I chose to go on the 'leadership track' when choosing lives. What is that? And why wouldn't everyone try to grab those fun lives?"

"Most souls do not want the responsibility nor have the confidence to be a leader," she answered. "On the other hand, you revel in it, so you chose to have lives as a leader."

With that, my latest reading with Brenda ended. My next step was to find Nicholas in the historical record. If I could learn more about Nicholas, I reasoned, perhaps I could find an answer to my question about how I could be a good soul such as Thaddeus and then do an about-face and be as evil as Nicholas. Since I knew that he had to have participated in Germany's civil war in the 1600s, I would start there. That war was called the Thirty Years' War, and it was widely known for the soldiers' pillaging of civilians.

# Chapter 19: Count Nicholas von DesFours, the Thief

*Know thyself? If I knew myself, I'd run away.*
　　　　　　　　　—Johann Wolfgang von Goethe
*Here an attempt is made to explain suffering: the outcaste of traditional Hinduism is held to deserve his fetched fate; it is a punishment for the wrongs he did in a previous life.*

　　　　　　　　　—Walter Kaufmann

## Reincarnation highway mile marker: Germany, seventeenth century

Most people do not like to study history, but I do. History is often stranger than fiction, and it can be just as entertaining. The old saying, "Those who forget history are doomed to repeat it," is definitely true. After World War II, when the horror of the Jewish Holocaust became common knowledge, people would ask, "How could the cultured and civilized Germans that produced Beethoven and Goethe participate in such a thing?" Almost everybody was unaware that the dress rehearsal for the Holocaust had taken place three hundred years earlier in Germany during a bloody civil war. But in that war, it was the Catholics and Protestants who were massacring and abusing each other. The Thirty Years' War was a horrible, deranged time, and it had a devastating effect on the German people. Historians have estimated that between one-fourth and one-third of the population perished from direct military causes or from the illness and starvation caused by the war. Overall losses were serious enough that historians believe that it took a century after the war for Germany's population to recover. It was truly a world gone mad.

When Brenda described Nicholas as a pillager, I knew that he had participated in this war and that its recorded history would be the place to find him. Another thing I now realize is that the Source did not reveal Nicholas's last name to me on purpose. The reason goes back to Chapter 16, where the value of surprise was discussed. Just before I became Frank, I knew everything that there was to know about Nicholas because I had lived that life. As Frank on earth, I have complete amnesia about Nicholas because we do not bring that kind of information down here with us. My challenge was to search for Nicholas on my own and receive the reward of satisfaction if I succeeded. After all, to be a member, you have to remember!

Information about the Thirty Years' War is easy to find. I started with the Internet, where I picked up the relevant fact that many nobles used the war as an entrepreneurial opportunity to get rich. How can that be? The online Catholic Encyclopedia explains that "German economic life, which for a long time had flourished greatly, had become stagnant. Consequently, there existed a large number of people who were glad to have the opportunity to support themselves as paid soldiers and to enrich themselves through plunder. The nobles, also, who were numerous in proportion to the rest of the population, took advantage of the chance to indulge in their private feuds and robberies. As only a small number of them were attracted by foreign wars, they were ready for internal disorders. Soon, there appeared leaders of ability who gathered both nobles and townsmen under their banners and retained them in their service by indulging their evil instincts. After reading that, I asked the Source if I had been one of those nobles, and I received a yes answer.

I got another clue from the Thirty Years' War Museum website, which described how these warrior nobles made money from the war.

The armies of the Thirty Years' War consisted of up to 40,000 mercenaries. Princes, however, had considerable financial and organizational problems recruiting them and providing for them. Therefore, independent war entrepreneurs were commissioned to raise regiments, who recruited men on their own. Profit interests prevailed clearly. Private bargains with suppliers, embezzled soldiers' pay, and cuts in provisions filled enterprisers' and officers' coffers. Often the only chance for common soldiers to survive was foraging through the use of force against the peasant population. Only higher-ranking officers could expect booty and glory. It was recognized that a regimental commander did not only need profound knowledge in mathematics, geometry, tactics, and engineering. He also needed the ability to keep up the discipline of his own regiment with an iron hand in order to avoid disorder in the battle and violence against the native population. These *entrepreneurs* of war often had raised their regiments themselves and had paid for the equipment in advance to be reimbursed later. When the army couldn't pay the wages, the colonel often paid the soldiers himself to keep them under the banners, waiting to receive what the army owed him later.

After reading that, I asked the Source if I had been a regimental commander who had raised a regiment. Once again, I received a yes answer. Now I had something to work with! I Googled "Nicholas Von regimental commander 30 years war" and, disappointingly, received no relevant information. I searched the Internet for a week and got zilch. The search was getting frustrating, so I switched gears. I knew already from my meditations that I had fought on the Catholic side (where else?) and that I had formed my regiment in 1625. The Catholics had two main armies. One was composed of Holy Roman soldiers led by Tilly, and the other was a mercenary army raised and led by Albrecht von Wallenstein. It didn't take me long to conclude that I must have been part of Wallenstein's organization. As it turned out, I reported directly to him. Wallenstein came up with the idea of raising armies and paying for them by extracting "concessions" (extortion money) from both friendly and enemy towns and cities. The emperor enthusiastically supported this proposal since he got the use of a large army without having to pay for it. Nicholas was one of many nobles to receive a charter from Wallenstein to raise his own regiment. But where could I find his last name?

I ordered two companion books from Osprey Publishing called *The Imperial Armies of the Thirty Years' War*. These books described in illustrated text the infantry, artillery, and cavalry units of the emperor's army. On page forty-three of the second book was a bibliography of nineteen books that had been used as resources. I asked the Source for a little help in determining which book would identify my regiment. "Would you help?" I asked, and I got a yes. I then went through the list and received eighteen negative answers until I got to the last book, *Der Geschichte der Wehrmacht, Die Regimenter ...*" by Alphons von Werde, printed in 1901. That book got the yes. *Where can I get a German book printed in 1901?* I wondered. Miracle of miracles, I found that Google actually had it online for free. I quickly downloaded it and opened it up. There was a convenient search feature, so I put "Nicholas" in the search box and pressed enter. A page written in German (of course) came up, but I could understand it. (See the next illustration.) Three imperial cavalry regiments had been established in 1625. To my utter delight and satisfaction, the regimental commander of the second regiment on the page was named Nicholas von Des Fours, who was identified as a baron. I asked the Source if I was this man, and I received an affirmative answer!

I had found my old family name—Des Fours. It sounded French. Later I would learn that it was and that its French meaning was "from the furnace." But if my name was Des Fours, where did that name "Putlinz" come from? I glanced to the regiment above mine on the page. *Oh, my God!* I thought. *My colleague commander's last name was Puttlinz!* Giving me the name Putlinz and then leading me to find it on the same regimental roster page was the other side's validation statement that I really had once been Nicholas von DesFours.

Now that I finally had my last name, I Googled "Nicholas von DesFours" and found more web listings. The first was on the German Wikipedia, which had the DesFours family tree, with my brother, Jean, and me heading the list.

Dragoner-Regiment
**Obrist Hebron.**

**Errichtung und nachgefolgte Veränderungen.** 1625 errichtet [1]; 1628 erst in Arquebusiere, dann in Infanterie umgewandelt und unterstossen [2].

**Regiments-Inhaber.**

1625 **Hebron**, Daniel, Obrist.

Regiments-Commandanten.
1625 der Inhaber Obrist Hebron. | 1628 Puttlitz, Obrist.

**Feldzüge.**

Hebron. 1625 stand das Regiment in Böhmen.
1626 bei der Belagerung von Kosel.
1627 in Polen und in der Mark.

Dragoner-Regiment
**Obrist Des Fours.**

**Errichtung und nachgefolgte Veränderungen.** 1625 in Böhmen geworben [3]; 1626 wahrscheinlich abgedankt und in das gleichnamige Arquebusier-Regiment eingetheilt [4].

**Regiments-Inhaber.**

1625 **Des Fours**, Nicolaus Baron (später Graf), Obrist.

Regiments-Commandant.
1625 der Inhaber Obrist Des Fours.

**Feldzüge.**

Des Fours. 1625 stand das Regiment in Böhmen.

[1] Chlumecky. Seite 47. Das Regiment hatte mit dem gleichnamigen Arquebusier-Regimente nur einen Stab. Siehe auch Cuirassier-Regiment Hebron, Seite 420.
[2] Chlumecky. Seite 48.
[3] Kaltwich, Aldringen, Seite 72 und 73.
[4] Waldstein wollte sie schon Juli 1625 abschaffen, doch bestanden sie noch im December 1625.

Google

*The regimental list displaying Baron Nicholas von DesFours as Obrist (colonel). Notice the name of Obrist Puttlinz as psychic validation above.*

Looking at the family tree, I learned some surprising facts. First, I had actually survived the war. I was born in 1588 and died on December 5, 1661, living to the ripe old age of seventy-three. I married twice, both times to countesses. I had four children, and the last, a son, created a Czech noble family line. After the war, it appeared that I had been a member of the royal court, serving on the Privy Council (a sort of cabinet to the Holy Roman Emperor). I also served as chamberlain, the highest-ranking officer in the court. Also in the family tree was information about my nephew, Louis, who was a canon at the Cathedral in Nancy, France. Brenda almost had it correct—the cleric was my nephew, not my brother.

*The family crest of the Des Fours family. Notice the cavalry weapon symbols from the Thirty Years' War and the Holy Roman Empire's eagle symbol.*

Well, so much for the positives of Nicholas. Now to the recorded negatives about him. For those details, I turned to the book *Wallenstein* written by Golo Mann. The hard copy that I received was, unfortunately, in German and more than 1,200 pages long. Nothing ever comes easy. In the "Officers" chapter, I found myself being singled out as an example by the supreme military leader himself. Unfortunately, it was the wrong kind, as I was described as the perfect example of a bully. Wallenstein said of me, "Des Fours is a plague. He caused more disturbance and robbery than the entire army. His last name means "furnace," and he was in fact as hot as one. Only someone of his conscience could possibly name Lt. Colonel Höffer as his second in command. Höffer was even more of a berserker than DesFours, if such a thing was possible. When Höffer was brought to me under arrest for court martial, DesFours made excuses for him, claiming he could not do without so many riders. I told him that he had more than enough."

Ouch! That hurts! As sanctimonious as my boss was about me, Wallenstein was not above selling me a castle that he had confiscated from the Protestants. I made so much money from the looting operations that I could afford to buy the famous Hrubý Rohozec castle in Czechoslovakia from Wallenstein.

The Hrubý Rohozec castle is an absolutely beautiful place set in what's called the Bohemian paradise. You can find many videos of the castle on YouTube, and many picture galleries showing its interior are also online. The castle grounds are very popular nowadays as a site for weddings, and many composers travel specifically to play and make recordings on the magnificent old organ there, a handful of which have been made into YouTube music videos. The castle is also a popular tourist destination; the Czechs give tours of it with tour guides dressed up in clothes from the period. It's one of those surreal moments for the present me to look at these videos of my old home. Of particular interest to me are the pictures of the war trophy room, which is dominated by a life-size portrait of a large bearded man in armor. Although the photo's caption does not mention the man's name, I know that it's me as Nicholas, the revered founder of the noble family that lived in that castle for three hundred years until it was confiscated by the communists after World War II. The Hrubý Rohozec castle is a perfect example of noble taste and gentility; none of the visitors there would have any idea of the base brutality that was behind the creation of the noble facade.

*Nicholas's Hrubý Rohozec castle, Czechoslovakia. Photography by SJu.*

What excuse could I have for the horrible regression from the pious Thaddeus to the plague Nicholas? That excuse would be the standard excuse that all bad high school boys use worldwide—"Everyone else was doing it!" I was both the founder and colonel of my regiment. As founder, I put up the front money to arm and equip my men. I was an entrepreneur risking my money. My charter allowed me to receive tributes from enemy towns and "contributions" from friendly towns to offset the expenses I occurred for service to my God and emperor. Of course, things did get out of control as time went on. Gary Brecher writes about those times as follows:

> Most of the dead weren't killed in battle. They died when the army that their local prince had put his bets down on lost. The soldiers on the losing side could flee—and they did, usually, with no delay at all, since they were mostly foreigners. But the villagers couldn't flee or they'd starve—there was no Red Cross for those peasant refugees. They had to stay while mercenary scum, just utter scum, sadistic at a level that would make Liberia look like a Quaker Teachers' College, poured into the farmlands and had themselves a good time in the name of whichever god and/or king they were paid by. Rape went without saying. Murder; standard practice, famine and plague was guaranteed once these filthy bastards swarmed through. After a while the soldiers got bored with ordinary killing and started using their imaginations; sometimes just to pass the time and sometimes to get the peasants to tell where they'd buried their grain or bacon.

The above writing makes me shudder. If robbery, pillage, and abuse were as common as described above and I was held out as an example of the worst of it, why wasn't I also court-martialed like my underling Höffer? The reason is that Wallenstein needed me. I was a good commander and an excellent fighter. History shows that my regiment distinguished itself as being excellent in the decisive battle of Lützen in 1632. In that battle, two of the oldest and most experienced infantry regiments of the enemy Swedish army were first decimated by imperial artillery and infantry fire and then ridden over by the charging imperial cavalry. Nicholas and his wild bunch were part of that imperial cavalry charge. So, I repeated my question to the Source. *What was my major sin as Nicholas?* Surprisingly, it was not the robbery or the rape. It was not even the battlefield killings that I committed. My sin was that I took seven lives that were not supposed to be taken. Those poor souls were supposed to continue living and working on their life lessons. It was not time for them to die, yet I killed them.

Who were these victims? I did not know anything about them when I originally submitted the manuscript of this book to the publisher; I only knew the number of them, 7. It was only after this book was close to being published that I did finally get the facts in a reading with Brenda. Brenda and I spent the entire hour long reading to obtain the following details:

Victim #1: Louis Des Fours, his nephew and Canon of a St. Georg cathedral, Nancy, France. Nicholas stabbed and killed him in a dispute over ownership of inherited land. As Louis was a clergyman, Nicholas was incensed that Louis would not turn over the land to help increase the power of the Des Fours family. To Nicholas' disgust, noble family pride was not important to Louis. With Louis' death, Nicholas obtained rights to the land.

Victim #2: Name unknown. In the 30 Year's War, Nicholas stabbed and killed a prominent citizen of the German city of Nuremburg when that man was attempting to protect his beautiful wife from Nicholas' advances. Nicholas had followed the women home and barged into her house in pursuit of her. Once Nicholas killed the husband, he then had his way with the wife as he originally intended.

Victim #3: Name unknown. The brother-in-law of Victim #2 was a newspaper publisher in Nuremburg. As publisher, he bravely wrote a scathing article about Nicholas' murderous behavior in his newspaper. Nicholas did not like the publicity, so he sent his riders to the publisher's office where they stabbed the publisher to death. To assert his dominance over the town, Nicholas raped the publisher's widow who was coincidently the younger sister of the first rape victim.

Victim #4: Name unknown, servant of Nicholas. Because of the looting operations that occurred in the 30 Years War, Nicholas obtained many bags of stolen coins in which he had to hide. One day he was looking for a specific bag of coins and could not find it. He accused a close servant of stealing it. He threatened the servant with a pistol to make him reveal where the missing coin bag was. When the servant could not tell Nicholas where the coin bag was, Nicholas shot and killed him. It turned out that Nicholas had temporarily forgotten where he hid that bag and remembered its hiding place only after he killed his innocent servant.

Victim #5: Name unknown, horse breeder. Nicholas was a regimental cavalry commander in the 30 Years War where he had the responsibility to ensure that his riders had good mounts. Cavalry units were continually in need of fresh horses to replace the ones that were lost in combat. However, trained horses were very expensive and these costs came out of Nicholas' own pocket. Nicholas had successfully purchased horses from this particular breeder before. However, in his very last visit to the breeder, Nicholas shot and killed him on his farm, his body falling into the river. Nicholas and his men then rode off with the murdered man's horses.

Victim #6: Name unknown, a subordinate Cavalry officer. Being a regimental commander in the 30 Years War was a lucrative position because of the looting opportunities. Nicholas' second in command, Lt. Colonel Höffer, was covetous of Nicholas' position of commander and plotted a mutiny. Nicholas found out about the plot and confronted Höffer which led to a sword fight and Höffer's death. Spiritually, Höffer is not considered one of Nicholas' seven victims because his death happened in combat. However, Nicholas then assembled the regiment and brought one of Höffer's subordinate lieutenants to the front of the assembly because he was involved in the plot. Nicholas had him tied up and then he personally tortured the lieutenant to death in front of all the men as a warning. The lieutenant is counted as the sixth innocent victim as Nicholas could have let him go instead of killing him.

Victim #7: Name unknown, suitor to Nicholas' daughter. Nicholas married his daughter, Marie Margareta to a Baron when she was 14 years old in 1658. This was obviously an arranged marriage that was common in those times. What is not in the history books is that Nicholas actually shot and killed the prior suitor to his daughter. Nicholas made a marriage agreement with this man and then broke it after he received a better offer from the Baron. The prior suitor made the mistake of not backing down after Nicholas renounced the agreement. With Nicholas' reputation, you would think that the original suitor would have used better judgment.

After receiving this information, my immediate reaction was one of being stunned. I thought, *I am not this man now, but I was him then, and it was only five lives ago! How much closer would my personality be to his if I had his body type instead of being smaller? If I did, would I still be out of control in this life?* That thought is something to ponder.

Staci Wells was absolutely correct in saying that I did not restrain myself or my men back then. I did not lead them to the higher good, which as Staci mentioned, is the spiritual goal of a good leader.

So let's return to the question—Why did my soul regress so badly? Remember when I previously stated that your soul shares control of your human body with a human conscience? It's like that analogy of an angel sitting on one shoulder and the devil sitting on the other, each trying to convince you of which way to go. Who will you listen to? In the case of Thaddeus, he was a gentle human and easy for my soul to nudge to goodness. Frank is reasonable as a human, and it's fairly easy for him to stay out of trouble. Nicholas, on the other hand, was just a mountain of testosterone and muscle. He's the equivalent of a nasty, snorting bull. My soul just could not control him, and he ran wild, doing what he wanted to do. Not being able to control your human body is not an excuse in the spiritual world. You are held accountable regardless of your efforts. No wonder most souls shy away from leadership lives. There are rewards, but there are also risks associated with the kinds of humans who are leaders.

So what's the penalty for committing the sin of prematurely taking seven lives? Well, obviously I did not go to hell because I'm writing these words now in Ohio, although I would say that my three years in Russia could qualify as a frozen hell. I discovered what my penalty was from a book called *Unfinished Business* by the famous psychic James van Praagh, who is one of the producers of the show *Ghost Whisperer*. He also gives public psychic readings to large groups. One of his recorded readings, which I will retell here, applies perfectly to Nicholas's sins.

At one public reading in California, Van Praagh noticed a spirit of a young man standing behind a woman in the audience. This middle-aged woman had come with two other women of the same age to Van Praagh's group reading. The three women were connected because they each had sons who were close friends in the late 1990s and who unfortunately died together in a fiery auto accident. The ghost of the young man was wearing a T-shirt with an image of a gun on it. In life, all three boys had been obsessed with the Vietnam War and repeatedly watched movies like *Platoon* and *Apocalypse Now*. (I certainly can relate to that obsession!) The spirits of the other two boys also showed themselves to the psychic. It was then that Van Praagh received the background story from the three spirits. All three had enlisted to go to Vietnam and had served together in a combat unit. One night during the Chinese New Year, they got drunk and came upon a car with a Vietnamese man and woman inside it. Just for fun, they started shooting at the car, and it unexpectedly caught fire. The Vietnamese couple, tragically, died in the car fire. However, nobody found out about this incident, and the boys went back to the fighting. In the end, none of the three soldiers survived the war; they were all killed in action. At the reading, the three spirits explained that they had a karmic debt going into their previous lives as teenage sons because they took life unnecessarily in their prior lives. The result was that in their life after Vietnam, they died in the car fire. One of the mothers asked, "But if they died in the war, didn't that even the score?" One of the spirits explained through the psychic, "No. As souls we planned to die in that war. As we took life unnecessarily, we had a debt to pay. Please do not feel despair because, by dying in that accident, we are now free!"

With my understanding of what happened during my life as Nicholas, rereading that story about the boys who died in a car fire made it clear to me why I had died violently in so many recent past lives. I had to pay Nicholas's karmic debt! I had to pay for seven lives, and I was actually close to paying off the bill. The past lives of Gorman, Konrad, Gustav, Karl, Alfred, and Otto offset most of the debt because I had not planned their deaths as exits. Do you remember Otto's last thoughts as he was floating to the white light after he died? He thought,

*I didn't see that coming.* Otto's death was a surprise to him. Unfortunately, Thaddeus's death by poisoning did not count toward the debt because that was a planned exit by my soul. But I finally had the answer I had been searching for. The only problem was that, at this point, I still had one more life to pay.

When I told Brenda about how I had connected my past-life deaths to Nicholas and how I had one more life to pay, she said something profound. She asked, "Are you willing to forgive yourself for that last death? After all, it's not God who judges us; it's our own souls who pass judgment on ourselves." I couldn't answer that question; I cannot speak for my soul. It will be interesting after the end of this life to see if my soul is willing to overlook this last owed life, assuming that I die naturally in this one.

During my normal meditation that night before bed, I was thinking about how lucky I was that I had been given the gift of being a psychic. I had no idea why I deserved this gift, especially with the sins of Nicholas staining my soul. The song "Amazing Grace" came to my mind, specifically the opening lyric, "Amazing grace, how sweet the sound that saved a wretch like me. I once was lost but now am found, was blind, but now I see." I then asked the Source why she had been so kind by giving me this wonderful psychic gift in light of my horrible behavior as Nicholas. In response, the Source spelled out the word L-O-V-E.

# Chapter 20: Father's Day

*If you don't believe in ghosts, you've never been to a family reunion.*
—Ashleigh Brilliant

*Here's something to think about: How come you never see a headline like "Psychic Wins Lottery"?*

—Jay Leno

## Reincarnation highway mile marker: USA, 2012

We are near the end of the reincarnation highway. The directions as to where to pull off of the road were, strangely, found at a local Mexican restaurant called Cinco de Mayo. What's relevant is the name. Because of my cultural ignorance, I thought it meant "the day of the dead." Every time I drove past the restaurant, I automatically thought of the wrong Mexican holiday. Nevertheless, good ideas can spring from misinformation.

The real Day of the Dead holiday is celebrated on November 1 and 2, when Mexicans honor their departed loved ones by sprucing up their graves and making offerings to their spirits. Although the celebration may sound morbid, it really is a celebration of the lives of the departed. The restaurant-inspired idea that grew in my mind was to celebrate my own, much improved version of the Day of the Dead. Previously, I lamented the fact that there were few positive attributes in the lives that were revealed to me. Maybe the reason was that I did not contribute to or do many positive things that could be remembered in those lives. In the life of Nicholas, he provided a castle for his family to live in for three hundred years. Perhaps I could also establish a valued legacy that could be handed down in my family. The gift I envisioned would be freedom from the fear of death for the generations that followed me. If all of my family could experience communication with the dead like I had, they would lose their fear and could live their lives differently. If we could have a successful group séance event, the memory of that event could be passed down through the generations. Who knows? Maybe sometime in the future after I am gone, my descendants could call me back for a conversation. To get the ball rolling, I was going to celebrate my own Day of the Dead. I considered the Mexican version way too one sided, as the communication was only from the living. My celebration was going to be a two-sided affair.

I decided to celebrate my new holiday on Father's Day 2012. I remembered the words of my father on his deathbed—he lamented that he would not be able to see how things turned out. His fear turned out to be unfounded, though, because, as a spirit, he did get to see what happened to his family. But his physical presence as grandfather was being missed by his grandchildren. I believe that the greatest gift that grandfathers provide to their families is their wise advice, and my children were deprived of this gift because my dad died much too soon. For my Father's Day present, I wanted my dad to spend time with his grandchildren so that he could give individual advice to each of them. I also wanted to include my teenage niece and nephew in this party so that all of my dad's grandchildren could have this opportunity. That was my audacious plan for my version of the Day of the Dead. Few human beings have ever tried such a thing, but I knew it could be done. To accomplish it, I scheduled a group reading with Brenda at the Mystic Nirvana for Father's Day weekend.

I specifically wanted my nephew, Brad, at the reading for a number of reasons. First, I knew that my dad had been very close to Brad when he was alive. Spirits choose whether to come to a psychic reading; they are not obligated to visit. They will come only if they are interested. I felt that having Brad present at the reading would cement our chances of having my dad show up. The second reason I wanted Brad there was that I was highly suspicious that Brad was a powerful psychic in his own right. I wanted to observe firsthand what his abilities were. My suspicions about Brad started four years earlier when Brad told me that he could see and hear his departed grandfather, Ernie, at his house. I learned of his visions before I started to meditate, so I really did not pay that much attention to his strange claim at the time, but now I was able to look at Brad's visions in a new light. After two years as a practicing psychic, I questioned Brad about what he saw and heard and came away convinced that he was not imagining things at his house. Brad's house would obviously have a strong connection to his departed grandfather, Ernie. My brother, Dave, bought the house from Ernie's estate, so Brad grew up in Ernie's house. Ernie loved to maintain the yard of this house; he actually died of a heart attack while cutting the lawn. Although Brad had never met Ernie—he was born a few months after Ernie's death—his visions were of his grandfather cutting the grass outside and of Ernie telling him that the heart attack hurt. Ernie would continue to visit Brad and communicate with him.

My confidence that Brad had psychic abilities was not based on his stories alone. I was becoming convinced that my dad's side of the family had a strong streak of psychic DNA. My awareness started with my grandfather Norm's (my dad's dad) recollections of his early childhood. He always had great stories, such as seeing John D. Rockefeller handing out dimes to children in front of his office building in downtown Cleveland in the early 1900s. More relevant would be his many ghost stories. For example, he recounted seeing his departed teenage sister walking outside their house just after her funeral. I was in my twenties when I heard these stories, and I just considered them amusing. I even took the effort to record them to tape, but I never believed them. Of course, my dad would just laugh at these stories when he was alive, but his brother and sister believed them because they had had their own paranormal experiences. Aunt Jackie claimed to have had out-of-body experiences to escape painful illnesses when she was a child. Currently, she complains of low spirits bothering her in her apartment, especially after Uncle John returned an old "birthing chair" that she had brought back from New York City. This birthing chair had supposedly been used in a New York City brothel, and legend has it that several deaths during childbirth occurred in its use. John was storing the chair for his sister at his house, but he got rid of it because too many strange bangs and other noises were happening at night in the vicinity of the chair. Once John gave the chair back to his sister Jackie, the noises and bangs transferred from his house and went right to her apartment. This was not John's only ghostly experience. My uncle recounted a strange night in his apartment when he was in his thirties, just after an elderly woman died in the neighboring apartment. Some entity made loud tappings on his walls and windows that moved around the room as if someone was walking its perimeter. After reviewing the ghost stories of the two prior generations and then considering my own, I saw that Brad's visions fit into the family history. Brad, along with my daughter, Jani, were now the fourth generation of my family that would experience paranormal events. But new events made it appear that they were not the only representatives of the latest generation to sense spirits. My sons Brian and Camy were starting to see things as well.

In one of my many readings with Brenda, she told me that one of my sons was also psychic. She said that he was going to be a nonbeliever in the psychic world until the ghost of a woman got "right in his face while he was sleeping." Brenda was unsure which of the boys she was referring to.

One morning during the spring of 2012, Camy told me that he woke up in the middle of the night and saw the translucent image of a women standing next to his bed. He had to look out of the corner of his eye to see her. This method of seeing spirits is very common; Tony, the massage therapist, said he did the same when he would see spirits in his therapy room. I asked Camy if he was okay and if the spirit had done anything to scare him. He said that the vision did not do anything to him, and he did not seem to be upset about it. I then silently connected to the Source and asked if a female spirit had visited him in his room, and the answer I received was yes.

During the following weeks, I repeatedly followed up with Camy, and he would occasionally report having seen the apparition at night. Then, one morning, Brian reported seeing the same apparition leaving my bedroom and going down the hallway. That was a surprising report coming from Brian, who had always declared that he did not believe in ghosts or psychics. Once again, I checked with the Source, and she confirmed that Brian had seen what he said he saw. The question then became, Who is this female spirit roaming the house? As Brenda had predicted this was going to happen, I assumed that this apparition was just a low spirit who was visiting. I should know better than to make assumptions.

Father's Day was fast approaching, and I started to put the final pieces to my plan into place. Step number one was to clear this whole crazy idea with Karol. Since it was my Father's Day, she gave her blessing despite her misgivings about bringing the boys. Step two was to contact my brother, Dave, about having Brad participate. My brother readily agreed to have Brad come down to Columbus to spend a week with us.

He was completely supportive of Brad's attending the group reading and was tempted to come down and participate himself. Unfortunately, Dave and my niece, Lara, could not make it. Step three was to contact my father. The group reading was scheduled for 12:00 p.m. on the Saturday before Father's Day. During my nightly meditation session on the preceding Monday, I contacted my dad and asked him if he would come to the family event. I received an affirmative response. Just for fun, I recontacted him in meditation the night before the event and gave him a code word to pass to me during the reading to validate the experience. I told him to give me the code word "orange juice" when I asked for it.

During the morning of the Father's Day event, things appeared to be warming up on the spirit front. At breakfast, Camy claimed that he saw his bedroom doorknob being turned by itself in the middle of the night. He believed that the mystery lady ghost had returned. After breakfast, we had to corral the kids to get ready for the noon appointment with Brenda. Also, we would be attending a graduation party after that. At 11:30 a.m., I asked Jani to go to a quiet place and ask my father if he was still coming to the event, and she came back shortly and told me that my dad said he would be there. At 11:55, everyone piled into the van for the two-minute ride to the Mystic Nirvana. As we were driving there, I told Karol to listen for the term "orange juice" to pop up sometime during the reading. I told her the background of the code word, and she was amused that I really expected the term to be relayed back to me. "We'll see," I said. "That's what makes this whole thing fun. You never know what's going to happen."

I pulled into the gravel parking lot behind the converted house that now housed the Mystic Nirvana. Brenda warmly greeted us at the back door of the covered porch. She was surprised as she watched the six people of my family group march in, as she typically gives readings to one person at a time. "It's a special Father's Day, Brenda!" I explained. "We are all here to visit my dad. We are not here for individual readings."

Brenda shook her head, laughing, and led everyone to her office. Since we had six people there, I suggested that we use her meeting room just outside of her normal reading room. She thought that was a good idea and set up a large card table up. Brenda took the chair at the twelve o'clock position at the table.

Brenda had started using a Mac notebook to record the reading so that she could send a digital copy to her clients. She was letting the kids listen to a recording in which she had captured a ghost's voice. In the recording, you could hear Brenda asking, "Are you playing with my hair?" A low, gravelly voice responded, "I did." The kids thought that was pretty cool. Then Brenda got down to business.

"Is it okay if I still go around the room to start?" she asked. What she was referring to was her standard warm-up procedure, in which she taps into everyone individually. I did not expect her to do all of that work, but I always defer to her.

"Sure, whatever you are comfortable with," I replied.

Brenda turned to Brad, concentrated for a moment, and said, "Someone is here in spirit, a younger woman. She is showing me quilted patches. She talks really soft. She said that she liked you very much. Do you know who this person is?"

Brad responded, "Yes, I do. That's my mom's cousin, Denise. She died in a car accident. She was always quilting."

I turned to look at Brad and saw that he had a look on his face like he was concentrating and even seemed pained. Brenda said, "She is touching your arm now. Do you feel that?"

"Yes, I do," responded Brad.

Brenda was homing right in on Brad's psychic abilities. She said, "You are constantly feeling these things, aren't you? You are constantly being touched, aren't you?"

"Yes," Brad responded quietly.

"Dude, you are strong," Brenda continued. "You are pulling in people who are not even family. It's like that *Sixth Sense* movie, where all the spirits are attracted to you because they know that you can feel it. What did you hear that scared you a few months back? A man's voice whispered in your ear, didn't it?"

"It was early in the morning, and I was sleeping," Brad said. "I heard someone whisper in my ear. I did not know who it was."

Brenda reassured him. "It's nothing to be afraid of. Don't be afraid. He did not mean you any harm. Now who is that man who looks like a pirate that you see?"

"That's my grandpa, Ernie. He was a cop, but he looks like a pirate to me."

Brenda changed course. "There's another spirit trying to get in here. He says he belongs to your family, but you never met him. He died young and in an unusual way. He says he does not want the family to forget about him."

Somehow Karol beat me to the punch. She turned to me and said, "That sounds like your cousin Ted."

I blurted out loud, "Ted, we never forgot about you. But hey, I thought you would be back down here by now." I was referring to the fact that he had been dead at that point for thirty-eight years, and I would have believed that he had been reincarnated already. Of course, I was showing my human prejudice about time and forgetting that there is no real time in heaven. Ted's response was funny, revealing, and all Ted. "Some of us are slow," he responded through Brenda.

Brenda then turned to Brian. "You don't like attention shown to you, do you? You are very particular about things, aren't you?"

Brian nodded his head.

Brenda continued, "There is a female spirit kissing you on top of the head. She is calling you by a different name. You have seen her before, haven't you? By your closet."

"Yes, she was close to my closet."

Brenda laughed. "See, you can't fool me. I know that you see and hear things. You just don't want to admit it."

Camy, who was to my right, tugged on my arm. "Dad, I see a woman standing between you and Brian. She has a hand on each of your shoulders!"

"Good job, Cam," I whispered.

Brenda then turned to me. "All right, where is your father?" We waited about twenty seconds before she said, "Oh, there he is! I had to look at him before he would come in."

"Well, you do remember that he always liked to make an entrance as a spirit!" I said to Brenda. I then addressed my father out loud. "Dad, I have brought your grandchildren here for you on Father's Day."

Brenda laughed. "He said 'Thank you!' even before you got that statement out."

I then said out loud to my father, "Were we talking last night?"

He responded through Brenda, "On and off."

"What was the code word I gave you last night?" I asked.

Brenda was struggling with the answer. I should have kept my mouth shut and been patient, but I blurted out, "It was something associated with Florida."

Brenda said, "I was making it too complicated to interpret. Does it have something to do with a color?"

"Yes."

"Like orange something?"

"Close enough," I said. "The code word was 'orange juice.'" I looked triumphantly at Karol, but she shook her head. She was not buying my triumph.

I turned away from Karol and said out loud, "Dad, would you give each of your grandchildren some advice? Starting with Brad?"

Brenda turned to Brad and relayed the message, "Always listen to that voice in your head as long as it's about love. If that voice says hurtful things, ignore it. But if it tells you to do good things, go ahead and listen."

To Brian, Brenda relayed the advice, "Let your mind think of things that no one has ever thought of. Don't be afraid to think of things that no one has ever heard of."

Brenda turned to me; I was also going to be the recipient of a message. "Keep doing what you're doing. He's real proud of you and all you have done over the past couple of years. He's proud of the man that you are evolving into, especially over the past two years. Although he thinks that you are little intense."

"Hey, I got that from you!" I laughingly complained to Dad.

Brenda turned to Camy and restarted her reading process with him. "Do you have allergies? Do you have asthma?"

Karol responded that Camy had had asthma when he was younger. I looked at Camy and noticed that he was speechless. He was blown away that Brenda knew this about him. "Some spirit turned your doorknob this morning, didn't it?" she asked.

Camy nodded his head yes. While Brenda was talking about Camy, I whispered to Brad to ask if he could see my father. Brad responded quietly, "He's sitting in the empty chair besides me."

Brenda then said to all the grandchildren, "All of you kids are open; you are all very spiritual. I hope that you are able to stay open." She then relayed my dad's advice directly to Camy. "When you think of picking a permanent lady, remember it's not always about looks. Make sure that she has a good heart."

Brenda then turned to Karol and told her that a male spirit was very persistent in trying to connect to her. "He says that his name is Roger." Karol then made an association to the father-in-law of one of her best friends who had passed a few years earlier. She had spent a lot of time with his family during her divorced years, and she became very close with both Roger and his wife. After that visit was over, Brenda passed a message to Karol from my father. "He said he loves you smiling. He wants you smiling a lot because it makes him smile. He always liked your face when you smile because your nose wrinkles up. He loves all of you and misses you all, but he's always around. He said, 'Thank you for loving my son. You are a great mother to my grandchildren.'"

I have to admit—I got a little choked up when I heard my father's kind words to my wife.

Brenda then turned to Jani and asked, "Do you sing? 'A songbird'—your grandpa calls you a songbird. It doesn't matter what you sing. You love being out by trees? Walking in the trees singing—your grandfather likes to follow you. When you feel chills going up your neck, that's how your grandfather makes himself known to you. You dance when you are alone in your bedroom, don't you?"

Jani looked embarrassed and responded, "Well, not really."

Brenda laughed and said, "It's okay to dance. Grandpa likes it when you dance when you are in your room. You crack him up. He didn't want Frank to know that he dances with you. He's glad that you cannot see him when he dances."

I responded, "Hey, Dad, it's okay! You never danced in life, so why not dance now?"

Brenda then passed my dad's advice on to Jani. "Always have fun, all through your life. If you do not have fun, you need to rethink your life."

Having completed everybody's readings, she asked if there were any questions.

"Brenda, who is that spirit visiting Camy by his bed?" I asked.

"Same one that is visiting Brian. I feel that she is your mother's mother." She turned to Camy and asked, "If I describe her, will you be able to tell? Does she have dark hair? She's not real short, a little taller than me, well dressed.

Camy could not say because all he had seen was shadows, but Brenda was describing my maternal grandmother, Naomi. I never expected that she was available to connect to because the information that I received was that my maternal grandmother and grandfather had reincarnated. I brought up that fact with Brenda.

"Even though they have reincarnated, it does not mean that they still cannot connect with you. The soul can split, remember?" explained Brenda.

That made sense to me. My grandmother always wanted to be with my children, and she was now spending time with them in spirit form. It was a wonderful surprise to learn that my grandmother was with me again. Then another wonderful surprise was given to me. Brenda asked, "Who had a big nose? There is a man here who is saying that he was known by his big nose. He's also making a cha-cha-cha kind of laugh, kind of like Jimmy Durante!"

"That's my grandfather!" I exclaimed. "I inherited my nose from him, and he always had that funny laugh. It has been so long that I had forgotten about the laugh." I was so shocked that he was there that I did not introduce him to his great-grandchildren, although I am sure that he was well acquainted with them on his own terms.

Brenda had another client waiting, so we had to get up and move on. Once again, I gave Brenda a big hug and warmly thanked her. Reconnecting with my long-lost grandparents made for my best Father's Day ever. We moved on to the graduation party, and Karol did not allow anyone to say anything about our psychic experiences to her side of the family. I thought that I would give the experience a day to settle in before I discussed it with my kids and Brad.

The next day, I met with my nephew alone in my office. I wanted to get his opinion of Brenda's reading and to make sure he was not upset from the experience. He told me that he enjoyed it and that he was fine. I then gave him some perspective on the psychic world and told him about the Source and how to connect to her. He listened intently and took in what I told him. I then asked him if we wanted to do a psychic exercise. He responded yes, and then I suggested that we both call my father down to the room we were in. Brad sat down in my overstuffed leather chair and closed his eyes. I went into a mild meditation and called out to my father. Just for fun, I usually use his airplane call sign, "29 Tango." I got an affirmative head shake that he would come and visit. I opened my eyes and looked at Brad. In a few seconds he said, "He said he would come."

"He told me that too!" I said.

My father's arrival took several minutes—*why* would be a good question. Was he involved in something else? Did it take time to undergo some transformation in order to communicate with us? After about five minutes of Brad and I just looking at each other, Brad suddenly announced, "He's here!"

"Where is he?" I asked.

"Sitting in the empty swivel chair."

"What is he wearing?"

"His yellow Windbreaker, the jacket that he would go flying in."

I swiveled my chair toward the empty third chair in the room and greeted my father warmly. "Hi, Dad. Welcome back. It's good to have you here."

I turned toward Brad for a response. He was sitting and concentrating with his eyes closed. I knew that he was straining to mentally listen for a response. Then he said, "He said, 'Thank you.'"

Taking the opportunity to use Brad as a medium just as I used Brenda, I continued the conversation. "Dad, Brad was saying that he has a hard time hearing you. Does that have something to do with the frequency he is able to pick up?" Brad said, "He's showing me a picture of a tall radio tower."

"From that picture," I said, "I will take it that what I said is correct."

Brad replied, "I thought I heard him say yes."

"Dad, if Brad meditated, would he increase his ability to hear you?"

"I heard a yes," Brad said, "and now he's showing me a picture of a Buddhist monk mediating."

"How many months do you think it would take him to improve?"

"He's showing me a picture of the number 2," Brad said.

"Two months?" I asked.

"He said yes."

Although Brad said that he had never heard my father before, he seemed to be able to hear him this time. "Dad, I miss not being able to see you, but I fear that my lack of ability to see you is because of the plan that was set out for me, in that I would not get all the psychic tools. Is that correct?"

Through Brad, Dad replied, "It's something like that."

"Will I ever get these gifts?" I asked.

Brad said, "He said, 'Keep doing what you are doing and you will be rewarded.'"

"So, Dad," I said, "the last time we communicated, you told me that you were hanging around Hawaii. Is that where you have been keeping yourself?"

"He said that he loves to fly in his Bonanza to different islands," Brad said.

I then jokingly chided my father, "Dad, you are in heaven and can have any airplane that you want. You can upgrade to an F-15 or at least a P-51 Mustang. Why would you stay with your Bonanza?"

Brad replied, "He's laughing. He said that he would never give up his Bonanza."

"Dad, I met a woman named Nanci Danison who had a near-death experience," I said. "When I told her that I did not want to come back to earth again, she told me that the grass is always greener on the other side. Where would you rather be—down here or in heaven?"

"He said where he's at now."

"But you will have to come down here again. How many more lives do you think you will have to live?

"He said that he has lived many lives," Brad said.

"I know that, but how many more lives do you think you will have to live?"

"He said about seventy-five."

"Yuck. I hate to sound like a malcontent, but that sounds horrible. Where would you really rather be?"

"He said that he would like to live out the rest of his time up there and just watch you guys down here."

"Dad, when you visit this house," I asked, "have you ever run into Naomi?" (That was my grandmother who was visiting the boys.)

"He said that he had and that he said hello to her. He said that he understood that the boys had seen her," Brad said.

"They did," I said. "It's nice that she's here with us. Were you surprised that your father-in-law showed up at Brenda's?" (I was referring to my grandfather, who was Naomi's husband and who unexpectedly showed up at the Father's Day reading.)

"He said he was surprised."

"Dad, are you aware of the name Nicholas von Des Fours?" I asked.

Brad said, "He said yes."

"Did I kill seven innocent people?"

"He said yes."

"I know I paid back six of those lives already. I still owe one life. Any chance I can be paroled from that last debt?"

Brad said, "He said that you already paid for that last life."

"I know of only six lives where I died violently and unexpectedly. What was the seventh life?"

"He said that your good works in this life canceled out that last life debt."

I addressed the empty chair where the spirit of my father sat and again joked with him. "Now, you wouldn't be part of a conspiracy on that side to make me drop my guard so that I could be plugged easier?"

"He's laughing," Brad said. "He said that he is not part of any conspiracy."

"You do know that I am armed to the teeth down here in this house. I was not going to go down easy." (I was referring to my real gun collection and ammunition that I have stored in my gun safe.)

"He says he knows."

I didn't realize this until I thought about it later, but I had never told Brad about the story of Nicholas von Des Fours. He was in no position to manufacture any intelligent answers to the questions about my past life that I was directing to my father. Since these were not Brad's answers but answers from the other side, our amateur reading was actually another validation that I had once been Nicholas.

My son, Cameron, was loudly playing video games on the big TV set in the next room, and the noise was starting to interfere with our psychic event in my office. To solve that problem, I asked my father if it would be okay to bring Cameron in on our conversation.

Brad said, "He said that he would love to hear his voice."

With that, I got up from my chair and went into the great room next to my office. I asked Camy to come join us. He sheepishly came in and went to sit down in the empty chair.

"Don't sit down there, Camy!" I said. "You will sit on Grandpa."

Camy looked bewildered and stood in the middle of the room, confused. I took him by the hand and had him sit on my lap.

"Cam, your grandfather is in the room just like he was at Miss Brenda's," I explained. "Why don't you ask him a question?"

"I don't know what to ask," Camy said.

"Can you see him sitting in that chair?"

"I can just see his legs."

"Why don't you ask him what you are going to do in your life?" I suggested.

Camy turned toward the empty chair and asked, "Poppa, what am I going to be?"

Brad said, "He said you are going to be very successful. Wait. He just disappeared, just like that!"

I thought for a minute and then realized what had happened. "Brad, was it just like someone yanked a telephone wire out of the wall and the connection was lost?"

"Yes, it was just like that!" Brad said.

"Boys, I think we just broke a rule. We are not allowed to ask spirits about the future. We did, and the other side cut the connection. We're going to have to be more careful next time."

With that, our Father's Day festivities came to a close. Once it was over, I decided that it had been a smashing success for me. Not only did I succeed in including my deceased father in a family activity, but I also reconnected with my cousin Ted and my grandmother and grandfather. That was a total surprise. Relatives whom I had loved and thought were lost forever actually came back. Father's Day changed my negative viewpoint of the reincarnation highway. The revelations of my bloody, violent prior deaths had ruined the glorious promise of immortality offered by reincarnation. Up to that Father's Day, my planned name for this book was *My Harrowing Journey down the Reincarnation Highway*. The reincarnation highway was "harrowing" to me because of my violent past lives. Take my bad deeds out of the equation, and the reincarnation system transforms into something wonderful, it allows everyone to experience worthwhile immortality. Worthwhile in that we would use our time to experience many viewpoints and to gain wisdom. As such, the events described in this chapter caused me to rename the book.

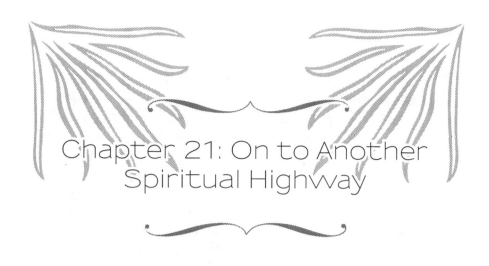

# Chapter 21: On to Another Spiritual Highway

*It appears that the purpose of the entire universe is experience—firsthand, gut-wrenching, personal experience. Nothing can replace it.*
— William Buhlman

## Reincarnation highway mile marker: The end of the current road

We have now come to the end of the reincarnation highway in the life of Frank. This is where we (me, the author, and you, the reader) both get off and go onto different roads. Before we part company, there are a few things I want to clear up. Shem said that we spend most of our current lives remembering the lessons of our prior lives. I wanted to give my opinion of which lesson and experience from Otto's life was most important for me in this life. I believe that it was the experience of successfully leading the remnants of my platoon during the January 1944 retreat in the snow. That experience really boosted my soul's self-esteem. It took a great deal of perseverance, but I did lead my men to safety and it was for their greater good. I believe that I then carried forward this esteem and confidence into my life as Frank so that I was able to tackle everything that was thrown at me. This answer also neatly answers the question, what does the dangerous life of a German soldier have to do with a suburban American businessman?

I thought that I was pretty clever drawing this conclusion, and I wanted to get Karol's opinion. One evening on vacation, when she was sitting on a porch rocking chair reading a book, I sat down next to her and told her this theory. I saw her face assume that skeptical look that I knew all too well.

"You mean that after all I shared with you, you don't believe that I was once Otto?" I asked in a surprised, almost exasperated tone.

"I believe in the spirit stuff because I experienced it for myself," she said. "But as far as being able to identify specific past lives, that's just too far out there. You took bits and pieces of things and stitched those stories together and ended up with the outcome that you wanted."

"But what about the validations of each past life? Otto's hometown of Mandeln, the Twenty-Third Regiment, and the Eleventh Division being geographically linked and historically accurate? What about Laurie's, Brenda's, and my own independent psychic revelations about Otto matching perfectly like a puzzle? What about the psychic group confirming Laurie's reading that Konrad was stabbed as a bishop? What about the "Puttlinz" name that was given to me months before I found that name on the roster of regiments that contained my old name of Nicholas Des Fours? Remember when I was given the name Nicholas and Brenda later identified him as a thief? Historical records confirmed that as fact."

"They are just coincidences, stuff that you just ran with," she replied.

"I can understand that if there was only one coincidence, you could say that. But I just rattled off at least five coincidences. This number of coincidences would be almost impossible to conjure up!" I responded.

"Sorry, I just do not buy it."

"But Karol, your own friend Linda said she was once a deaf French girl, and we met Iris on vacation in Jamaica, who told me she had actual memories about being General Cornwallis's mistress! I am not the only one who has found his past lives."

"Sorry, you heard those stories; I didn't," replied Karol.

I wasn't angry with Karol; I was just amazed at her inability to see what I did. When I shared my past-life stories with Asian-Indian friends, they accepted it without even a raised eyebrow. In fact, they seemed happy that my experiences were validating their own beliefs. But when I heard Karol's final judgment, I realized that Western cultural beliefs are so firmly entrenched that my reincarnation experiences would be automatically dismissed out of hand by most readers of this book. However, Karol did admit to accepting that spirits exist and can be interacted with only because *she experienced actual communication with spirits*. That was the key; most readers will accept what was presented in this book only if they experience it for themselves. To be honest, I would believe the same if I was in the reader's position.

If you are spiritually curious, I leave you now with a choice. You can either move on to other amusements or find out for yourself what exists on the "other side." You certainly do not have to; just as Michele's priest said, "All will be revealed to you after you die." But if you don't want to wait for that, it does not cost anything to meditate. You never know what you will find. If you have any trouble, just sincerely ask the universe for help, and it will be provided. I promise. I hope you can see what I gained through my journey; I know who I am. I understand completely what my current life was and is about. I am now completely grounded.

What road will I take from here? I decided that I will try to find the on ramp to an even more exciting spiritual highway. The very night that Karol discounted my past-life experiences, I downloaded a book on my tablet reader called *Adventures Outside the Body* by William Buhlman, who found *everything* that I found on the reincarnation highway and more. The only difference in method was that he explored the other side through out-of-body experiences instead of through psychic means. I was amazed that Buhlman's background was very similar to mine. He started out life as an atheist, and his experiences led him to find God in the universal consciousness, as I did. He also discovered that he too had been a German soldier in WWII who died on the Russian front. (Maybe dying on the Russian front is a soul's ticket to enlightenment, using Laurie, Buhlman, and myself as examples.)

Why would I now try to pursue out-of-body experiences? Remember, heaven is not a place but a higher vibrational experience. If I have an opportunity to go there through this method, I would be crazy not to try. Many folks believe it is dangerous or scary to leave your body and explore different dimensions, but I am not worried. I was a cavalryman in at least two of my past lives. It's in my soul to ride out and scout the unknown. The potential payoff is huge. Buhlman was extremely successful in his out-of-body journeys, just like Robert Monroe was. Both of their experiences were fantastic. They met deceased relatives and other kind spirits. They also visited fantastic landscapes and experienced bliss and ecstasy. Leaving your body and going on day trips is not easy to do, as it does take practice and preparation, but I believe my meditation skills will give me a head start. Best of all, the spirits assure me that I will finally see and hear on those journeys. The other side has been giving me nudges to pursue this new road, so they will not have to ask me twice.

In once again pursing out-of-body experiences, my journey has come full circle, back to the beginning. Recall that I started to meditate just so that I could have such an experience, but my one out-of-body experience led me to the psychic world and reincarnation. The gift I received from the reincarnation highway is that I will start my new quest not fearing death. I recall the comforting words of Karol's deceased Italian grandmother, Noni, who told me during a Brenda reading that there is no interruption of consciousness during and after the death process. She said, "It's as easy as turning your head. *Itsah* nothing to worry about!"

# Appendix 1: Funny Psychic Stories and Deleted Scenes

Many movie DVDs have a great feature that allows viewers to see filmed scenes that were edited out of the final product. This appendix is just like that. When I started my spiritual journey, I thought it would be mostly a psychic adventure, and I never thought it would center on reincarnation. I had a number of funny psychic stories to share, but they did not fit into the story line of reincarnation and so were not included. I will take the opportunity to share them here. Besides being amusing, they reveal some very interesting secrets of the other side.

## Bo-Bo the Wonder Dog and Clairaudience

Throughout this book, I have whined about not being able to see or hear psychically. It seems that in this system, if I want to hear or see anything psychically, I am out of luck. However, if the "other side" really wanted to communicate with me, then all of the sudden I will have the ability to hear for their convenience. Here's the story about how I briefly obtained this ability. I have a house that is on a sloped lot. This feature lets me walk out of the lower level of the house and into the backyard. One half of my backyard is lawn and the other half is wooded. The back property line is defined by a four-foot-wide creek that's about three inches deep during normal times. At the time of this story, BoBo the wonder dog was still a puppy, but he was starting to become adventurous. I had put up a short chicken wire fence up in the shrubbery and the wooded areas of the backyard to keep the dog in the yard. I did not fence in the creek side because the dog was afraid of crossing the water and I did not want to make the effort. On this particular sunny summer day, I was alone with BoBo in the backyard; Karol and the kids were off someplace. BoBo ran off into the wooded portion of the backyard and I followed after him. He went to the creek and then summoned up the courage to cross it. That little devil, I thought, as I had to chase him down and carry him back into the patio section of the backyard. It was at this point that I saw something amiss on the patio that required that I run in and grab a tool. I thought that the tool I needed was on top of my workbench. It should take only fifteen seconds for me to grab it. *Should I take the dog in with me, or should I just run in real quick?* Typical guy that I am, I just ran into the house with a warning to the dog to stay where he was. I ran to my workbench, and, of course, the tool was missing. I dug through my toolbox with no success and walked over to a shelf to look there. I was starting to get worried about the dog when I heard a voice inside my head clearly say, "You'd better attend to your dog!" *Crap!* I thought. I knew exactly what had happened, and I also knew that what I had just heard was not my mental voice. A guide or God herself was snapping me to attention. I ran out of the house and, sure enough, the dog had disappeared. Our house is on a corner lot, so I ran to the street to cut him off. When I got to the street, I noticed that a car had stopped in the road, and I saw a woman standing beside her car holding Bo-Bo. I went up to her and retrieved the dog with many thanks to the kind woman. Boy, that was close! If something happened to that dog, I would be in huge trouble with my family. After I got the dog back into the yard, I thought, *Oh, that's what clairaudience sounds like!* It seems that Bo-Bo the wonder dog has divine protection. I never told Karol this story until now.

## Danger during Brenda's Psychic Lesson

After Brenda created the Mystic Nirvana, I went to one of her Thursday night psychic classes. On this particular night, it was packed; there were at least twenty-five people there. The exercise that Brenda had selected for that night was psychometry, which is the ability to make relevant associations between physical objects like keys, watches, and rings (anything really) and their owners. For example, Brenda claims that you could count the number of scratches on the watch and get a relevant fact about its owner. To do this exercise, everyone would put a small object of his or hers into a bowl, and then each person would randomly draw an object from the bowl to work with. Each person would then have to give a reading about the owner of the object that he or she selected. I had never really bought into this concept, so every time I did this exercise, I would cheat. I would just ask my guide what the object owner's story was. I just did not want to count scratches and dimples. The object I selected that night was a bracelet. I plugged into one of my guides, and the message I got was *run*. As the bracelet was a woman's, I knew exactly what that message meant. Whoever she was in this room, her current romantic relationship was not a good one and she should leave it. The only problem was that in the room, there were at least two couples. Brenda had stated that the rules of the exercise were that you had to give your reading before the owner of the object would be identified. There was no way I was going to tell the owner that the other side suggested that she leave her significant other if she was sitting right next to her significant other that night. You never know how guys will act, and I did not feel like duking it out that night with a younger, bigger guy. When it was my turn to give my reading, I stood up and announced to the group that I would not give this reading without knowing first who the owner of the bracelet was. Brenda protested that it was cheating. "Sorry," I said, "for reasons that you'll see, I need to know first. Okay, who owns this bracelet?" A very pretty young blonde, who had come alone that night, raised her hand. *Whew! I am safe!* I thought.

I asked her, "Are you in a serious relationship now?" and she replied, "Yes, I am." I said, "Sorry, but for what it's worth, the other side is saying that you should run from it."

Later that evening, I was able to talk more with the young woman. She told me that she had previously gone to a psychic who had told her the same thing. After that night, I never saw her again. I wonder if she took the advice from the other side to heart.

## Soul Colors

During psychic lessons, Brenda would have participants give practice readings to one another. I was, of course, at a disadvantage because of my slow download rate of psychic information compared to that of others. To give a quick reading, I learned how to read how far a person's souls had advanced. That was something that I could do quickly and that no one else had figured out how to do. I got this idea from the book *Destiny of Souls* by Michael Newton. On page 171, Dr. Newton describes how a soul's advancement can be determined by what color the soul shows in its aura on the other side. New souls start out as pure white and then, as they gain wisdom through living lives, they turn different colors. Dr. Newton came up with the below rough chart from his studies:

| Step | Soul Color | Role | Level |
|---|---|---|---|
| 1st | White | Beginner | 1 |
| 2nd | Off-white | | 1 |
| 3rd | White and reddish pink | | 2 |
| 4th | Light orange yellow | | 2 |
| 5th | Yellow | | 3 |
| 6th | Deep gold | Student guide | 4 |
| 7th | Green or brown green | Guide | 4 |
| 8th | Light blue | Master guide | 5 |
| 9th | Deep blue | Master guide | 6 |
| 10th | Deep blue with tints of purple | Master | 6 |
| 11th | Purple | Ascended master | Higher level |

Using this chart, I could quickly give someone an interesting reading that would determine whether he or she was truly an "old soul." What's even more fun is that I applied this chart to some of our current political leaders. I think you'd find the below chart interesting as far as how advanced some of our political leaders are.

| Soul Color | Role | Level | Examples |
|---|---|---|---|
| White | Beginner | 1 | |
| Off-white | | 1 | Bill Clinton, Michael Moore, Adolf Hitler |
| White and reddish pink | | 2 | Josef Stalin, Barack Obama |
| Light orange yellow | | 2 | George W. Bush, JFK, Nancy Pelosi, Richard Nixon, and Newt Gingrich |
| Yellow | | 3 | George Bush Sr., Jimmy Carter |
| Deep Gold | Student guide | 4 | George Washington, Abe Lincoln, Ronald Reagan, FDR, and Mitt Romney |

I don't know about you, but the above chart explains a lot of things to me! That was so much fun; let's do that again with the people from this book.

| Soul Color | Role | Level | Examples |
|---|---|---|---|
| White | Beginner | 1 | |
| Off-white | | 1 | |
| White and reddish pink | | 2 | |
| Light orange yellow | | 2 | Julie, my first wife |
| Yellow | | 3 | My dad, Brenda, Michele/Lana, Dave, and Karol, my second wife |
| Gold | Student guide | 4 | Staci Wells, yours truly, Tony, and Linda |

I guess that I am going to go into training when I get back to the spirit side!

## Psychic Directions

As an experiment and for use as a handy tool, I use clairsentience to find things and people. The first time I tried it was to find my lost car keys at home. Unlike my wife, I would drop my keys in multiple locations in the house and then lose track of them. One time, my keys were missing for two days. I had to use my wife's copy, and it really bugged me that they did not turn up quickly. In frustration, I asked the Source for help. I called out mentally the rooms that I thought the keys could be in, and I received head-shake answers in response. *Great room?* No. *Kitchen?* No. *Laundry room?* No. *My bedroom?* No. *My bathroom?* No. *My walk-in closet?* Yes.

I walked into my closet and saw no keys. Then I realized that the last time I had them, I was wearing a pair of shorts that were now in the dirty clothes hamper. I looked in the hamper, and sure enough, there they were. Thanks, spirits!

Another time, I had a mesh bag of ten tennis balls that I was using in a baseball skill exercise with my nine-year-old boys. We were going out to the practice field across the street, and I realized that I had forgotten another piece of sports equipment in the house. I ran back into the house and went downstairs to get the equipment. Just like my car keys, I absentmindedly put down the bag of tennis balls somewhere. I went outside and realized that I no longer had it, so I went back to the house and just could not find the bag of balls anywhere. The next day, I was still amazed that the bag of balls was still missing. I just could not find it in the house. Just for fun, I decided to try the psychic search method again. I connected to the Source, asked for help, and mentally called out the rooms again. *Upstairs great room?* No. *Lower level?* No. *Laundry room?* No. *Garage?* Yes. *On the storage shelf?* No. *By the shelf?* Yes.

I walked out to the garage and started to walk to the storage shelf by the back wall. On the way to the shelf, I nearly tripped on the tennis ball bag, which was on the garage floor next to the car. Thanks, spirits!

Okay, how about using this psychic tool to find a person? On a trip to Legoland in California, two of my kids were in a long roller-coaster line. My wife and one of my sons were not going on the ride, and they were sitting down waiting for the other two kids to go on the coaster. I walked away to do some scouting, and when I came back, the two kids were still stuck in line and my wife and other son had gone someplace else. Just for practice, I wanted to find them psychically. The technique I used was to physically point my finger in a direction and wait for the head-shake response. I would keep moving my finger in twenty-degree increments to the right until I got a yes. I would then move in that direction until I came to a point where another choice had to be made and then repeat the process until I found them. Following the directions of the spirits, I found Karol sitting behind a short wall about 125 yards away. Not bad! Thanks, spirits!

Another time that I did this trick was on top of a volcano on the island of Maui. During spring break, we had taken the kids to the Hawaiian Islands. We had a great time at the beach, but I really wanted to show them the top of a dormant volcano. We jumped in the car and made the drive to the top. The views were breathtaking, but the wind was sharp and the temperature was in the upper forties. Jani was wearing her favorite yellow horse baseball cap, and when she got out of the car to look over the edge of the cliff, a gust of wind grabbed her cap and blew it into the lunar landscape below. She was absolutely distraught. When we were finished taking in the view at the top, we drove a little bit down the road to another observation point. The parking lot was very close to the base of the cliff that her cap had been lost from. As she was still crying about it, I promised her that I would try to look for it. The air was pretty thin as we were at ten thousand feet, and I was feeling a little short of breath. I thought that it'd be a great time to ask the spirits if they would lend assistance. They agreed to do it. While I was stumbling along the base of the cliff, I had noticed a large lava rock that was curled like the top of a dairy queen ice cream cone. I thought it was pretty cool looking, but it was way too big to haul out of there. While I was looking for Jani's cap, I kept an eye out for a smaller version of that lava rock so that I could take that one home. In the meantime, I used the same search technique that I had used at Legoland. The spirits took me all over the place until I came to a chain-link fence. I could go no farther. I thought that the spirits were playing a trick on me. "Thanks a lot, guys!" I said, laughing. *Oh, well*, I thought. I had given it my best, but it was time to turn around and walk back. On the way, I saw a lava rock that was kind of interesting, and I picked it up and took it with me. I did not examine it closely. When I got back to the car, I told Jani that I had not been able to find her cap. But to mollify her, I told her that the volcano spirits had told me that they wanted her to have the rock that I was carrying in exchange for her cap. I gave her the rock, and she examined it. Her eyes lit up, and she exclaimed, "Thanks, Daddy! This rock is shaped just like a horse's head! This is really cool!" What can I say but "Thanks, spirits!"

Speaking of Jani, she also has psychic ability. This was demonstrated on our last stop on our California vacation. We stayed at a beautiful Napa Valley inn nestled among the vineyards. To pass the time on a flight or riding in the van, my kids play on handheld game devices. Being nine-year-old twins, they were prone to misplace them. My wife was always scooping them up in the wake of the kids and saving them from getting lost. In fact, Brian lost his Nintendo DS on top of that volcano we visited in Hawaii. Anyway, upon leaving our hotel room for dinner one night, Jani realized that her blue Nintendo DS was missing. We searched the room and the rental van with no luck. Jani was once again in tears and distraught. We stopped the van outside the inn's lobby to see if it had been turned in. Karol got out of the van to go to the lobby, and I stayed in the van with Jani sobbing profusely. To distract her and quiet her down, I suggested that she psychically connect to my dad and ask him where the lost toy was. She calmed down and closed her eyes. Thirty seconds later, her eyes popped open, and she told me that my dad had told her that the game was close by. That calmed her down a little bit. At dinner, my wife and I decided that the device was probably lost when the kids exited the van at a gas station. I guess that showed my lack of faith in Jani's psychic abilities. The next morning, Karol found the toy buried deep in a plastic souvenir bag. It had been close by after all. Thanks, Dad!

*The "horse" rock from the volcano.*

## Eagle Road

Do you know that I actually belong to a church now? I go occasionally to the Guiding Light Spiritualist Church on Morse Road in Columbus. A spiritualist church service is very similar to a Christian service except that there are no crucifixes and the congregation believes in reincarnation. Oh, and did I mention that the reverend is psychic? In fact, the piano player and one half of the congregation are psychic! It's the perfect church for me. My favorite part of the service is the psychic readings at the end. The piano player is an elderly black lady named Cindy who is a beautiful soul and who just beams love, if such a thing is possible. During one service, Reverend Joe gave a great sermon and then announced that it was time for messages from the Spirit. Cindy turned from her piano on the stage and said that she had something for Frank. She closed her eyes and said that she was seeing a white pearl.

"Does that mean anything to you?" she asked.

"No, not really," I replied.

"No, wait. They are telling me it's Pearl Road. It's off of I-71. They told me to tell you not to get off on Pearl Road. I see you driving on the exit ramp and reaching for a drink. You will not see that car in front of you by the gas station. They keep saying, 'Get off on Eagle Road instead!'"

"Wow, I do get off on the Pearl Road exit off I-71 when I go to my office in Cleveland. Luckily, I have no plans of going to Cleveland this month. Do you mean *Engle* Road instead of Eagle Road? Engle Road is where I stay overnight when I go to Cleveland. It's the next exit past Pearl."

Cindy responded, "Could be Engle. Just do not get off on Pearl Road! You'll be going there soon."

I thanked Cindy and told her that I would be careful. Sure enough, the next day I learned about a software problem that I had to fix in my Cleveland office. You can be damn sure that when I went to Cleveland that very week, I did not get off at the Pearl Road exit! As a matter of fact, I would not get off at that exit for three months, and I was real careful when I did.

## Karol's Soul Name

When I read the *Journey of Souls* series of books by Dr. Newton, I noticed that all the spirit guides had special soul names. By inference, everyone would have his or her own soul name. I wanted to find out what my soul name was, so early in my meditation practice I asked about it. Back then, I didn't know about low spirits, and one of them pulled my chain by telling me that my name was Indio because I used to be Mayan. I thought that was pretty cool. A few months later, I wanted to find out what Karol's spirit name was, and the answer I got was *Kem. Hey, that's pretty cool!* I thought. It took me about thirty seconds to realize that KEM were the initials of her full maiden name. *Ha-ha, pretty funny, guys.* It was my joker spirit guides up to their old tricks again.

## Sinusitis

One night in the spring of 2012, I was doing my normal presleep meditation. When I got into a meditative state, I asked my normal question, *Any messages for me?* Like I said before, nineteen out of twenty times, the answer is no. However, that night, I got a yes. *Okay, what's the message?* The answer I got was in the usual riddle form—a word that starts with an *S* followed by an *I* and that has nine letters. In my meditative state, I could not work out the riddle. *Rats!* I was tired but also too curious to let it go until the morning because I often forget the whole clue by the time I wake up the next morning. I dragged myself out of bed and went to my computer. Some websites will give you a list of possible words if you put in the first letter and the number of letters it could contain. I entered "word starts with *S* with nine letters" into Google and looked at the results of potential answers. I went through the word list and mentally asked, *Is it this one?* of each word. I got continual negative responses until "sinusitis" was answered with a yes. Having a narrow Italian nose and allergies, sinusitis is a malady I suffer from occasionally, but I was not at the time. *Am I going to get sinusitis soon?* I asked. I received a yes answer.

Two days later, a flu bug was raging through my family and the staff at the store. First, Camy got it, then Jani, and then Karol. I was waiting for my turn with apprehension. Sure enough, two days after my sinusitis warning, I came down with a queasy stomach, fatigue, and a bad headache. I announced to Karol that the flu bug had gotten me. I took two aspirins, laid down on the sofa, and took a long nap. The rest of my family had taken naps when they had this illness, but they would wake up not feeling better. I, however, woke up from my nap and did feel better—not 100 percent but definitively better. I then went outside and took a little walk. When I came back, my eyes were puffy from the pollen, but my queasy stomach symptoms were gone. Then I realized that I did not have the flu; I had sinusitis. Thanks for the heads up, Source!

## My Brother Dave Visits with the Other Side

My younger brother, Dave, is six years younger than me. To give you an idea as to what he is like, his cell phone ID on my phone is "Dave the Rave." I still introduce him to women as "fun Dave." He is truly just a fun-loving guy, and women just gravitate to him. We both got divorced about the same time in 1989, and Dave and I spent time together chasing women in downtown Cleveland for the next five years. He was a legend among my group of friends for his—let's say—social abilities with the opposite sex. Many times on a Friday night, I would go home at eleven o'clock, but he would stay out alone and then regale me with his stories the next day about what happened after I left. Eventually, I settled down with Karol, but Dave continued on with his merry ways. However, without his trusty wingman (me), he eventually hit a dry patch socially and got involved with Brandi. She was petite and attractive, but she was kind of a hard woman, definitely not his type. She was high-strung and had zero sense of humor. Of all the women that he dated, she was the absolute last person I would have guessed that he would marry, but he did. Eventually, Dave bought a house, had two children with her, and settled down into unhappy domestication. Like a wolf chained up in a small yard, he would look past the fence at the outside world and wistfully reminisce about happier times out in the wild. Maybe he should have paid more attention to what was happening *inside* his yard. In his fourteenth year of marriage, something happened.

One day in the fall of 2009, Dave called and told me that he thought that Brandi was having an affair. Later, his suspicions were confirmed. He just did not know what to do. He didn't want to be married to her anymore, but he did not want to get divorced. He did confront his wife about his suspicions, but she denied everything. He was not ready to face the hard reality that he needed to make the strong effort to either turn his marriage around or end it and become a single parent. What Dave missed in life at that point was the good counsel of our father. Our dad would always push Dave to make the right decision. I tried to counsel Dave the best I could, but I did not have Dad's talents. One day, inspiration hit me—why not have my dad resume his old role from beyond the grave? After all, I had had a pretty good conversation with my dad the prior month with Brenda. Why not do it with Dave? When I first told Dave about my reading session with our father, he was very intrigued, and his interest increased when I told him about Karol's experience. When I offered to facilitate a reading for him, he took me up on it, so I called Brenda and set up an appointment. I want to stress here that I in no way told Brenda why my brother was coming to see her, nor did I give her any information about him.

The morning of Dave's reading, I did some meditating to see if I could get the name of the spirit guide assigned to Dave. I did this so I could ask for his help that day and so I could see if Brenda would be able to identify the same guide's name. I was testing both my psychic ability and the degree of collaboration that the other side would allow in this effort. I was able to make contact with an entity that identified himself as Dave's guide, and when I asked him to spell his name, the response was Kai. I thanked him and told him that I looked forward to hearing from him later that day.

Dave drove down to my house from the Cleveland area and then we both went to the Mystic Nirvana, where Brenda greeted us warmly. I told her that this reading would be for Dave but that I would be in the room observing. She led us to her small, dark reading room with a card table and a lit candle. Brenda then went into her warm-up routine, in which she psychically learns about the subject. She told Dave that she thought he was a thrill seeker and that she saw him flying airplanes for fun. Dave confirmed that he was learning to fly airplanes and that he had just recently soloed in an airplane. Brenda then said that she sensed that Dave was having some trouble with a romantic relationship, which she knew because a female spirit was sitting in his lap with her arms draped around his neck. Although Dave could not feel anything, he smiled at that idea. Then we had a surprise visitor to the room. Brenda said that a Spanish lady with bright red lipstick and a nice dress was dancing around the room. Dave and I looked at each other, puzzled. Brenda then said that the spirit said that Dave had always been her favorite and that she was there with Sally. Brenda marveled, "She sure loves to dance." It then clicked with me. "That's not a Spanish woman," I said. "That's an Italian woman! It's Inya, our great aunt!" Our aunt had died only a few years before. I had a recent memory of watching an old home movie in which Inya was dancing a polka with Sally, my grandmother's neighbor. After our aunt left the room, I asked Brenda if she could connect with Dave's guide. In a moment or two, Brenda said that an African chieftain in full tribal dress had entered the room and claimed to be Dave's guide. He was holding a spear and forcefully slammed the butt end of it into the ground, saying that Dave must make a decision. The spirit guide then showed a picture of an African hut in an enclosure and said that Dave should leave the enclosure. I interpreted out loud that the enclosure idea might have been referring to the fact that Dave had bought Brandi's parents' house after her father died, and that house was in the same neighborhood that Brandi's brother and mother lived in. The enclosure symbolized the neighborhood that Dave lived in, and the spirit was recommending that Dave move away from that house. I asked if that interpretation was correct, and Brenda said yes. I asked Brenda what Dave's spirit guide's name was, and she replied, "I'm getting Kay or Kii, or something like that." I smiled and said that's what I had gotten as well.

Next, Brenda said, "Your Father just came in the room, and he's sitting at the table. He's pounding on it with his fist, and he's saying, 'Make a decision!'" She then said that Dad was sitting there with his uncle and that my dad was wearing one of those pink rubber wristbands, this one saying, "Your drama is your alcohol." Brenda said that Dave needed to move past the drama and get on with the decision at hand. I later interpreted that to mean that he needed to stop paying attention to where Brandi was sneaking off to and to focus on the more important matters. With that, the spirit of my father left the room.

There was one more spirit visitor after that. Brenda said that an older gentleman had come in the room and was telling Dave that he was his boss from the bakery where Dave had worked as a teenager. I knew nothing about this; I turned to my brother and asked him if he knew who it was. Dave smiled and said that it was his old boss, Bob, whom he had worked for at the Parma Bakery when he was in high school. The spirit apologized through Brenda to Dave, saying that he regretted not taking more of an interest in his employees. He said that Dave was a good worker. I personally was stunned that a spirit would apologize for such a minor thing thirty years after the fact. Dave later reminisced that Bob wasn't a bad guy to work for, just demanding and a little bit crabby.

When the spirits left the room for good, Brenda predicted that in a year's time Dave would be much happier and that he would meet someone with brown hair who would be a lot of fun. With that, the reading ended.

Dave and I went to a restaurant for lunch and to debrief. I was amazed at how accepting and nonplussed Dave was about the experience. He thought that it had been great and came away determined to move on with his life.

Through the encouragement of the spirits, Dave did move on. He moved Brandi and all of her things out of their bedroom and into the basement. He then filed for divorce. Brandi quickly tired of sleeping in the basement and moved out on her own in the spring of 2010 without her children. Brandi and Dave were divorced in October 2010. Because his children did not want to leave the neighborhood, he did not move his family from their house. Instead, he bought out his ex-wife's equity in the house and stayed there. In November 2010, he met a brown-haired woman named Chrissy, who he said was a lot of fun.

## Spirits at the Yacht Club

I belong to the Buckeye Lake Yacht Club, the oldest inland lake yacht club in the country, but it's by no means pretentious. It's very low-key and a lot of fun. One Saturday, I attended a big meeting of the members because I thought that the State of Ohio was going to announce plans for Buckeye Lake. Instead, the topic was about funding new retaining walls for our club. While I was sitting in the meeting, my crown chakra lit up. It felt like someone was putting a heavy crown on my head. When that happens spontaneously, I know that there is a spirit around me.

Mentally, I asked, *Someone here?* Yes. *Are you an ex-member?* Yes. *Welcome back! It's good to have you here! What is the first letter of your first name?* L. *Larry? Lonnie?* No. No. *Were you an officer here?* Yes. *What year?* 1978. *Will I find your name on a plaque in this main room?* No.

The spirit then faded away. After the meeting, I went over to the pool and asked a grandmother where I could find pictures of officers from 1978. She told me to go to the commodore's room where there are pictures of the officers from each boating year. I went to the room and found the 1978 group picture of officers. The only officer with a first name that started with an *L* was Lou McClain. I asked the Source if this was the man I was looking for and received a yes answer. Next, I had to find out if he was still alive to verify my discovery. I asked one of the current officers if he knew Lou McClain, and the officer answered that he had died a few years before and then he asked me if I knew him. I had the sense not to tell him that I had just made his acquaintance.

The next time Karol was at the club, I took her to the commodore's room, showed her the 1978 officers picture, and then told her the story of how I met him. "You are spooky!" she said.

"No, I am spiritual," I replied.

## Dreams

Most people have no idea what dreams really are—your personal connection to your soul and the spirit world. I know this to be true because I did an experiment on the subject. Here is what I found out.

Your soul never sleeps. During the day, it shares control of your human body with your human consciousness. At night, though, your human consciousness sleeps but the soul stays awake. During REM-stage sleep, your soul really steps out and goes into a higher vibrational frequency. At this stage, dreams occur. You have likely noticed that most dreams are strange and don't make sense. The reason is that the soul communicates in symbolism, just as spirits do during psychic readings. The dreams you remember are told in symbolic imagery. The soul goes through the events of the preceding day and retells them to you in symbolic language. That is why they seem so strange. While in this REM stage, the soul can be communicated with on a spiritual communication frequency. As a psychic, I can tap into this frequency and actually connect to the souls of living people while they dream. I got the idea of connecting to nonpsychics while they were dreaming from the book *Journeys Out of the Body*, by Robert A. Moore. Moore performed countless self-experiments in the area of out-of-body experiences and wrote at least three books about this subject. One of the chapters of *Journeys Out of the Body* inspired me to experiment with dreams. I found the results of my experiments to be amazing.

My ex-wife, Julie, and I occasionally e-mail each other. She found me through the LinkedIn website. As I had just started experimenting with dreams, I thought of a good test. I had forgotten the name of the company that Julie was working for, so one night, I woke up at about five o'clock in the morning, which would be two o'clock Julie's time, and asked Spirit if Julie was dreaming. I got a head shake yes in response. Just as I would ask to be connected to a spirit guide, I asked instead if I could connect to Julie. I received another yes answer. *Hello, Julie*, I said mentally. *It's me, Frank, visiting you in a dream. How are you doing?* I got a head shake affirming that she was doing fine. Now, was this a low spirit or was this really Julie? To determine this, I asked Julie mentally to spell out the name of her company. The entity on the other side of my communication spelled out an unusual name that started with an N. The next morning I checked out that name on the Internet, and it turned out to be exactly correct. I really had connected to Julie's soul while she was dreaming!

To push my experimentation farther, I wanted to find out just how much a soul in a body remembers about its prior lives. The ideal test candidate would be Michele because we had that prior-life connection. One night, I made a psychic dream connection with her and asked if she remembered her life as Lana. I received a no in response. I then asked her if she believed we had shared a prior life together, and once again she responded no. I thought that answer was profound. It appears that, when a soul is placed in a body on earth, both the body and its soul have amnesia regarding prior lives. I found out later that the reason for this is that the universe always wants to give everyone a fresh start when they work on their life lessons down here. I thought that a soul would, in the dream state, at least remember that it had lived prior lives, but at least with Michele, it appears that is not the case. I also thought that the soul would realize that it was in a dream state, but it doesn't seem to. I next asked Michele what she was doing at that moment. Using yes and no questions, I was able to get her to communicate that was she was sitting in her living room. I found it amazing that she had no idea she was dreaming in her bed.

The third example was an experiment I did to see if I could contact someone I had never met before. I chose President Obama as the subject. (Hey, why not go big?) One night, I was able to connect to him and ask him a series of questions about his real political beliefs. Let's just say that he is much more of a radical then he admits to publicly.

The purpose of sharing the dream experiments with you is to show you that everyone is connected on a psychic level. Even nonpsychics reach this frequency when they are dreaming. Just as I can connect to individuals in their dreams, spirits can easily and often do use dreams to connect to you. If you recall, my spirit guide Morton grabbed my soul during one of my dreams and then yanked me out of my body.

## Kurland

Even though I never wanted to bring a dog into my house, BoBo the wonder dog has been a wonderful vehicle for my spiritual growth. I guess that makes up for the messes he leaves in front of my office door. BoBo was instrumental in the beginning and the ending of this story."

It was a warm afternoon in the fall of 2011, and I was walking BoBo up a sloped sidewalk by a parkway near my house. BoBo's ears pricked up as he sensed two dogs in a group of people who were approaching us. This group of people included two walking children, another in a stroller, one teenage nanny, and one grandmother. They were obviously traveling to the park across the street. BoBo is friendly with all dogs, so he enthusiastically greeted the two dogs. As the three of them socialized playfully, the grandmother complimented me on how handsome Bo-Bo looked, speaking with what sounded like a German accent. *My* ears perked up at the accent, and I couldn't help myself. I responded in German. *"Sind Sie Deutsch?"* (Are you German?), I asked.

In German, she replied, "Nein, Ich bin von Osterreich. (No, I am from Austria.) Bist Du Deutsch? (Are you German?)"

"Nein, Ich bin ein Amerikaner (No, I am American)," I answered. "Are these your children?" I was seeking a chance to compliment her through a joke.

"Nein, Nein. Ich bin ihre grossmutter (No, no. I am their grandmother)," she responded, still in German. "Du spricht gutes Deutsch! Wieso?" (You speak good German. How so?)"

*Oh boy, how do I answer her?* I thought. I knew that if I told her the truth, she would think I was crazy, but something told me to go for it.

"Glauben sie an reinkarnation? (Do you believe in reincarnation?)" I asked.

When she responded, she switched to English. "Not really," she said, "but you never know."

Choosing to continue in German, I replied, "I war ein Feldwebel in der Wehrmacht. Ich starb am 1. Mai 1944 in Estland (I was a sergeant in the Wehrmacht. I died in Estonia on May 1, 1994)." I then switched to English. "I died on the way to the Kurland Peninsula."

"My father was also in the Wehrmacht," she said. "He was captured at the end of the war at Kurland."

Now I knew why I was having this encounter with this woman! What were the odds of this happening? There are no coincidences, remember?

"I am very sorry. Did he come home?"

"No, he died in the Russian prison camps," she said. "I was a young girl, and I never saw him again."

"I want you to know that he was a brave man," I said. "Army Group North was the last unit to surrender; they were never beaten. If he lasted to the end, he had to be a very good soldier."

With that, the conversation shifted to her son, who was about my age and lived in a house two streets away. She told me I should look him up as he spoke German too. I said that it had been a pleasure to meet her and invited her to stop by my house and visit.

As I walked away, I realized that her father would have worn a Kurland cuff band, the same kind that I had on my gun wall. I also recognized that this nice woman probably had nothing to remember her father by. At least with the US Army, a deceased soldier's personal effects would be sent back to the family. When a soldier was on the losing side, as the Germans were, that courtesy was not extended, especially with the Russians. It then hit me that she might appreciate my Kurland cuff band. I went back to the park to find her, but I was unsuccessful. And because my memory is now shot, I had completely forgotten what her son's name was, so I could not look him up. But I knew that she lived in the Cleveland area, so I decided I would keep a sharp eye out for her in the future so I could give her my gift.

Fast-forward to the following spring. One evening, I was out taking Bo-Bo out for another evening walk. I was walking up that very sidewalk where I had encountered the Austrian grandmother, and I mentally renewed my wish to run into her and give her the military decoration. If you have learned anything from this book, it would be, "Ask and you shall receive." I turned around and headed for home. When I got to the front of my driveway, I noticed a middle-aged couple walking across the street and said hello to them.

The man replied, "I think I am supposed to talk to you."

"Really?" I said. "Who are you?"

"You talked to my mother last fall in German," he said. "My name is Ralph."

"Guten Tag, Ralph," I said. "Wie gehts?" (Hello, Ralph. How are you?)

"Gut," he answered.

You notice that I really was not surprised by this encounter; I had asked for it only five minutes before. It had obviously been arranged by our good friends on the other side. I was grateful for the opportunity, and I grabbed it.

"Ralph, I have something that I want to give to your mother," I said. "Would you have time to stop in?"

He and his wife agreed to come into my house, and I took them down to the gun room. Ralph had recently become a hunter, and he was amazed at the gun collection. I pointed to the Kurland cuff band on the wall and told him that his grandfather would have worn one like it and that I really wanted his mom to have it since she did not have many keepsakes of him. I took it down and handed it to Ralph. He was touched and gratefully accepted my gift. He told me that his grandfather had been sent to the Russian front as punishment for showing kindness to some Jews and Gypsies who were on their way to a concentration camp. All that his family had to remember him by were photos and a few letters. Hearing this story made me feel even better about the small gift I was giving. Ralph's mom obviously had not told him about the crazy reincarnation story that I had told her. He then asked, "How do you speak German so well? Is your family German too?" *Now what do*

*I do?* I thought. *Aw, what the hell!* In front of the gun wall, I told him a truncated version of the story that I have shared with you in this book. He and his wife seemed to enjoy the story and expressed an interest in reading the book when it came out. Ralph's father had been in the Hitler Youth in the war, and he wanted to bring him over to see my collection. "Absolutely!" I said.

With what transpired over the past three years, I can say that my World War II obsession is now over. Been there, done that! I will not sell the gun collection, but I do look at it as being my past and no longer my present. When I originally obtained the Kurland cuff band, it was a validating symbol to me because I had once died on the way there, but I had not earned it. It really belonged to Ralph's family. I was honored to give it to them.

# Appendix 2: Defending the Faith

This is the only philosophical part of this book. It's not meant to upset anybody; we are just talking here, exercising our brains, if you will. We are pushing the boundaries and testing ourselves. I am not trying to convert anyone because it truly does not matter to me what your spiritual beliefs are. In this appendix, I wanted to take the information that I learned from my journey down the reincarnation highway and try to answer some age-old philosophical questions. You may not agree with my answers, but if you are honest with yourself, you will see that they do seem to answer the age-old paradoxes.

Sometime in 2011, the *Columbus Dispatch* ran a review of the book *The Case against God: A Lawyer Examines the Evidence* by John E. LeMoult. I read the review and immediately thought that the book would have been *my* kind of book before I took my spiritual journey. Ironically, it had the same title as the book that got me into my original trouble with Michele. With the newspaper clipping in hand, I got a sudden intuition. *Do you want me to counter this?* I mentally asked the Source in response to the intuition. I received a surprising affirmative answer. I hung the clipping on my posting board for future reference. I did not buy the book then, although I knew that it would be well written with perfect logic. That newspaper clipping hung on my posting board for months until I finally took it down, as I did not see a way of working the information from that book into this one.

To close this book, I want to answer the age-old question "Why would a loving God allow pain and suffering?" As I started to organize and think about this appendix, I realized that this book had come full circle, back to Chapter 1, where I could now take the place of Michele in arguing for the existence of God—not that it is important to me to convince anyone that God exists. However, intellectually, it would be fun to defend my newfound spiritual viewpoint. John LeMoult also used the "Why would a loving God permit pain?" argument to help support his viewpoint, I saw that there was a connection between our two books. A great challenge would be to answer the tough questions that LeMoult's and the first *Case against God* book asked. Could I succeed in this argument where Michele's priest had so dismally failed? However, Michele had to defend her point of view only against the atheist viewpoint. I realized that to adequately defend my viewpoint, I would *also* need to defend myself against the Christian side, whose natural tendency was to believe that I was communicating only with demons. I would have to fight the dreaded two-front war that the Germans always seemed to fall into. To take on this challenge, I have set up a fictional trial in which I would be cross-examined by a team of two prosecuting attorneys—Mr. Jones from the atheist side and Ms. Smith from the Christian side. I hope that going through this exercise might help to answer any questions that you have after reading this book. Following is the imagined transcript of my testimony in this trial.

## TESTIMONY OF FRANK MARES, A MEMBER OF THE GUIDING LIGHT SPIRITUALIST CHURCH

**Mr. Jones: Do you believe that God does, in fact, exist?**

Frank: Yes

**Mr. Jones: Do you believe that God is all powerful and all loving?**

Frank: Probably yes for the first, and definitely yes as far as loving.

**Mr. Jones: Do you believe that Jesus Christ was the son of God?**

Frank: Yes, just as much as you and I are the sons of God.

**Mr. Jones: What do you mean?**

Frank: God is a strong energy force in the universe that also happens to be self-aware. All self-aware creatures in the universe derive their consciousness from this universal self-aware energy force. As such, you and I could be considered children of God.

**Mr. Jones: Do you believe that Jesus Christ died to save man from sin?**

Frank: No. I believe he did earthbound souls a service by creating Christianity. Using myself as an example, the establishment of the Christian religion allowed me to have the rich, meaningful lives of an archbishop, an abbot, and a mercenary who fought for the Catholics. The Catholic Church's belief system even gave me the opportunity to lose my first girlfriend in my current life. Christianity has touched countless souls in many ways.

**Mr. Jones: What was the purpose of Jesus's crucifixion and death?**

Frank: As my mentor, Staci Wells, might say, he was dramatically expressing his own truth as a soul. Only by his dramatic sacrifice could the religion of Christianity be established and grow.

**Mr. Jones: How could a loving God want a human being to undergo this horrible form of torture and death?**

Frank: In short, a person's soul chooses this horrible abuse; God has nothing to do with it. (See the end of this appendix.)

**Mr. Jones: Do you believe that only people who believe in Jesus Christ are allowed to go to heaven?**

Frank: Regardless of religious beliefs, everyone's consciousness goes to a higher vibrational frequency, commonly called heaven, after the death of the body. Heaven is not a physical place but rather a higher vibration of energy. Consciousness is a form of energy, and the laws of physics say that energy cannot be destroyed.

**Mr. Jones: Do you believe that the Bible is the literal word of God?**

Frank: No, but it does have a spiritual purpose.

**Mr. Jones: Do you believe that God created the earth in six days?**

Frank: No. I don't know if God created the Big Bang or if the Big Bang created God. At my low station in the universe, who or what created earth and the universe has no effect on my current life.

**Mr. Jones: How can a loving God permit one group of people to conquer, slaughter, and commit genocide against another group of people?**

Frank: I do not believe that God operates this way at all. In a universe with 140 billion galaxies containing at least two billion stars each, Earth is not the sole home of intelligent creatures with self-consciousness. However, of all the homes to civilizations in the universe, Earth is the toughest to survive on. Human conflict is a big part of the survival challenge here. From throughout the universe, souls come here to test themselves and to learn under harsh conditions. And while under the handicap of these tough conditions, souls are supposed to show courage and unconditional love to other souls. Souls make the choice to undergo this tough test; God does not compel them.

**Mr. Jones: How could a loving God allow so much evil in the world?**

Frank: Evil is relative from person to person. God lets us have free will so that we can test ourselves. As souls, we do not have to be here on earth; we choose to come here. We can go to other places in the universe that are far easier. Using an earth analogy, most normal people would not ride a bull in a rodeo, but some brave people do ride bulls for the challenge of it. I think they're nuts, but that is their choice. Most souls in the universe believe that souls who go to earth are nuts too, but it is their choice. They can quit at any time.

**Mr. Jones: How can a loving God permit horrible birth defects in infants? How can they possibly show unconditional love under such circumstances?**

Frank: That's the whole point of the exercise. They are trying to show courage and unconditional love despite their handicaps. Souls actually volunteer for these lives as an ultimate test. They are truly brave souls. I would suggest that you read Chapter 3 of the book *Courageous Souls* by Robert Schwartz. This topic is directly addressed there.

**Mr. Jones: Why doesn't God stop the devil from doing evil on earth?**

Frank: Simple—because there is no devil or hell.

**Mr. Jones: Some theologians argue that the world is only six thousand years old. Do you agree?**

Frank: Absolutely not. Fossil records show that *homo sapiens* have lived for almost 220,000 years. I also have a great fossil collection from the creek in my backyard, with the pieces coming from the Devonian period. These fossils are over 350 million years old.

**Mr. Jones: Do you believe the doctrine of creationism or that of intelligent design?**

Frank: I believe in evolution, although God as an energy force may have nudged the process.

**Mr. Jones: So, by inference, God could have designed man and everything about him?**

Frank: I have no idea, but she says that she did.

**Mr. Jones: What do you mean by that?**

Frank: I am a psychic, remember? I have the ability to ask the universal consciousness questions, and it responds to me with information that I never possessed before.

**Mr. Jones: Can you prove that you are a psychic?**

Frank: Not scientifically, but if you read my book, you will see that I document a lot of instances in which the probability of my obtaining the information that I received randomly or by guessing is infinitesimally small. So I am a liar, a mental case, or a psychic. There is at least a 33 percent chance that I am right.

**Mr. Jones: As a so-called psychic, can you tell me my future right now?**

Frank: It does not work that way. Future events are revealed to someone only if it would help that person achieve the life mission that was set out by his or her soul. For example, Brenda Posani did accurately predict events in my life, but the purpose was to establish credibility with me so that I would go on with my spiritual journey.

**Mr. Jones:** I will now turn the questioning over to my associate Ms. Smith.

**Ms. Smith:** Mr. Mares, you have stated that you receive information from the "other side." How do you know with whom you are communicating?

Frank: I don't, really, since I cannot see or hear who I am communicating with. I can only evaluate the source of the information by the nature of the information given.

**Ms. Smith:** How do you know that you are not communicating with demons?

Frank: Once again, I can only evaluate by what was said. However, everything that was communicated to me for three years actually reflected deeply held Christian values. Examples would be Shem, the Native American chief who encouraged everyone to show love; the deceased baker, who was apologetic for not being more interested in the lives of his employees; and my father, who emphasized that he should have focused more on relationships than money. Other examples are the deceased Uncle Don and Grandma Miller, who complimented my wife for the good work that she was doing and wishing her well. At no time was there any encouragement to break the Ten Commandments or undermine the good names of other people to cause dissention. The messages were totally about love.

**Ms. Smith:** The devil is the ultimate trickster. How do you know that his scheme with you is not to trick people into forgetting that the only road to salvation is through Jesus Christ? By listening to you, people would lose their salvation by hearing false words of love.

Frank: First of all, the devil does not exist in the spirit world. And logically, the whole concept of the devil in Christianity makes no sense anyway. For example, if the devil is the opponent of God, why would he severely punish people for joining his side? If he did punish people in hell for breaking God's rules, then he would be God's enforcer and, therefore, on God's side. Logically, he has to be on one side or the other; he cannot be on both.

Second, your question ignores the fact that Christians make up less than one-third of the world's population. If you believe that God is all loving, then you must believe that a loving God would not automatically condemn 66 percent of the world's population because they do not follow Jesus Christ. Either God is all loving or he is not. There is no logical middle ground. As such, the spiritual view of giving unconditional love to others would not cause an *all-loving* God to condemn someone for solely following this creed.

**Ms. Smith: How can you claim there is no devil, or Satan?**

Frank: Throughout my three entire years of psychic activity, reading spiritual psychic books, and having personal exposure to gifted psychics, no spirit or psychic ever brought up any communication or experience with demonic beings. There were encounters with mischievous low spirits who sometimes do bad things but nothing to suggest the existence of an organized evil force in the universe. There is only the Source, who told me that the devil, or Satan, does not exist. Man does a more-than-sufficient job of doing evil things without the help of a being intent on facilitating evil actions.

**Ms. Smith: If you believe in God and seemingly have all the answers, why do so many religions exist?**

Frank: The creation of many religions sets up the perfect test for souls on earth. Despite our many religious differences, we are supposed to rise above them and show unconditional love to others who have different religious beliefs.

**Ms. Smith: Our Christian Bible specifically forbids any contact with the spirits of the dead. For example, Leviticus 20:27 says, "A man or woman who is a medium or spiritualist among you must be put to death. You are to stone them; their blood will be on their own heads." And Deuteronomy 18:11 reads, Let no one be found among you who is a medium or spiritualist or who consults the dead." We believe these words to come from God. So if the Bible forbids "psychics," so to speak, how would you expect any Christian to accept someone like you?**

Frank: I think you just proved my point. Most of the world's religions struggle against one another—Jews vs. Muslims, Muslims vs. Christians, Hindus vs. Muslims, and now your question suggests Christians vs. Spiritualists. This is a problem we all must overcome by accepting our differences and having faith that all religions will be reconciled on the other side.

## END OF TESTIMONY

Would I have won my case? Well, I think that my fictional testimony made sense and was logical. You may not agree with my answers, but at least I *have* answers to the paradoxes that many religions cannot answer. But can I prove that what I said is true? No, I cannot. Why? Because, as LeMoult correctly states in his book, you cannot prove that the soul or the "other side" exists. I know the soul exists only because I had an out-of-body experience and because I communicate with spirits. Like the spirit of my deceased father said, "I don't have to believe when I already know." But as the vast majority of people never have these experiences, they must either have faith that the soul exists or disbelieve. The existence and the nature of the soul are extremely important in answering the question, "Why does God allow pain?" If you do not believe the soul exists, my answer will not make sense to you and I obviously would not score any debating points with someone like LeMoult. But if you do accept that the soul exists, here is my response to that vexing moral question about God and pain.

Before arriving at the answer, we first must change our perspective about human life. In other words, we must do a little "out-of-the-box" thinking. Let's start. If you lived only one life and had only one shot at it, that one life would be extremely precious. If some misfortunate event ended that one life badly, it would be a very cruel tragedy. However, the information that was revealed to me shows that we live many, many lives. Our conscious energy force jumps from body to body over time to gain many experiences and perspectives. As you have many opportunities at life, losing one to misfortune is not as significant because you can easily "sign up" for a new one. As a soul that can exist for eternity, you can take your time and experiment, knowing that you can have an unlimited number of lives to experience. Pardon the expression, but human life almost becomes cheap when you can experience as many lives as you want for free. Remember what the Buddhist monk told me in Niagara

Falls? "Don't worry about your past lives. They are just dreams." To a soul, they would be.

The second perspective to change is the concept of who we really are. Since you are born into your current life without any memory of your prior lives or of the time that you spent in that higher vibration known as heaven, you can see yourself only as a mortal human. That is your only perspective, and it distorts reality for you. However, let's assume that Christianity is completely correct, for the sake of argument. And let's say that you live for eighty pious years and then, after your death, spend the rest of eternity living in heaven. When you are in the Christian heaven, you have obviously left your body on earth, so you would be a spirit, a conscious being without a body. Since you will spend eternity in heaven and only eighty years as a human, would you be considered a spirit or a human overall? The answer is obviously a spirit; you were human for only a tiny portion of your existence. Using a similar analogy, a frog spends a few months as a tadpole and the rest of its life as a frog. What is this creature known as? It's known as a frog, the form that the creature spends the longest time in. In the reincarnation system, you are always a spirit and only sometimes a human when you have a human body during incarnation. Therefore, you should really consider yourself a spirit or a light being, not a human being. Being a human is only temporary. What's my point? Human life is only temporary, but spirit life is forever. Why would it be God's responsibility to prevent bad things from happening in human life? What would be the point of it? It's all a matter of perspective.

Let's consider another example. You are an environmentalist who deeply loves nature and all creatures. You appreciate the important job that the lowly earthworm performs, and you also love birds. One day in the park, you witness a robin capturing a worm to eat. That event is obviously a major tragedy for the worm, but as a human watching, would you ever intercede on behalf of the worm? You certainly have the power, but I am sure that the answer is no. You may love nature and all of its creatures, but you also understand how nature works. You would let the robin be and let things take their course, just like God does.

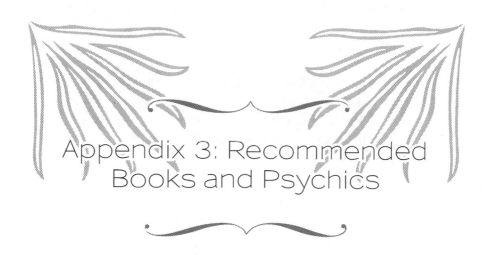

# Appendix 3: Recommended Books and Psychics

*Books*

1. *Life after Death* by Deepak Chopra
2. *The Spontaneous Fulfillment of Desire* by Deepak Chopra
3. *Backwards* by Nanci L. Danison, revealing the true purpose and our real relationship with the Source (God) from a woman who died and came back with a message
4. *Journey of Souls*, *Destiny of Souls*, and *Memories of the Afterlife* by Dr. Michael Newton, revealing the mechanics of the spiritual society in heaven and how reincarnation works
5. *Your Soul's Plan* by Robert Schwartz, revealing how you plan your life before you are born and providing a chance to see my life-plan mentor, Staci Wells, in action
6. *Earth School 101* by Alan Arcieri
7. *Unfinished Business* by James Van Praagh
8. *Do Dead People Watch You Shower?* and *Do Dead People Walk Their Dogs?* by Concetta Bertoldi
9. *Journeys Out of the Body*, *Far Journeys*, and *Ultimate Journey* by Robert A. Monroe, the late pioneer who wrote about his experiments in "out-of-body" travels and the fantastic things that he discovered in the spirit world
10. *Adventures Beyond the Body* by William Buhlman

*Psychics*
1. Brenda Posani, my psychic trainer and past-life mentor: www.mysticnirvana.com
2. Staci Wells, my life-plan and past-life mentor: www.staciwells.com
3. Frank Mares, visit my website and blog at www.reincarnationhighway.com